THE TITUS TEN

J. Josh Smith

THE TITUS TEN

FOUNDATIONS *for* GODLY MANHOOD

B&H
PUBLISHING
BRENTWOOD, TENNESSEE

To my one and only son, Josiah.
You are a living testimony to the healing
power of God. May you, like your namesake,
follow the Lord with all your heart, soul, and strength.
I love you, son.
(2 Kings 23:25)

ACKNOWLEDGMENTS

THIS BOOK HAS been written over the past thirteen years in the context of many men's groups. These groups not only helped me formulate these thoughts, they also gave me a vision for what God can do with men who are willing to trust and follow Him. Because of that, I am so grateful to the men of MacArthur Blvd. and Prince Avenue. This book exists because of you. May God continue to raise up many more like you!

Doug Nix, your prayers, support, encouragement, and insight were critical in helping me get these thoughts onto paper and finishing this book. You are a dear friend and I am so grateful for you.

Taylor Combs, thank you for all of your editorial work, encouragement, and affirmation along the way. This book is dramatically better than it would have been because of all your time and effort. Well done!

And to Jake Johnson, spending time with you has given me great hope for the next generation. I love you like a son and I am so proud of the man you are becoming. Remain faithful!

CONTENTS

THE TITUS TEN

WHEN I ACCEPTED my first senior pastor position at the age of thirty-two, I had no idea what I was doing.

I am a fourth-generation pastor on both sides of my family, I had been a full-time missionary, and I had been on staff at a large church, but none of that seemed to prepare me for the role of the senior pastor. It was overwhelming.

After about a year of trying to navigate this role by myself, it became abundantly clear that I needed help. Specifically, I needed the help of godly men. I not only needed their practical help; I needed their wisdom. We didn't have the financial resources to hire more staff, so I had to find these men within the congregation.

This growing sense that I needed the help of godly men coincided with the death of a few men who were founding members of the church. These were men I had gotten to know in the first few months of my pastorate. They told me stories about the early days of the church, when there wasn't enough money in the offering to pay the pastor so they took money out of their own pockets to pay him. They told me stories of coming to the church on Saturday evening to clean for Sunday morning. They even told me about going door to door in the community selling bonds to raise money for their first building. These were men who had given themselves, in unbelievable ways, for the good of the church. But these men were dying. And I didn't see any younger men taking their place.

I began to pray fervently that God would help me know how to raise up leaders from within the church who would carry the burden with me—men like those founding members. After a few months, I decided to begin taking men through the book of Titus. I asked ten men, ranging in age from early twenties to late eighties to give me ten weeks to walk through the book of Titus together. I called the group the Titus Ten.

After doing this twice a year for a few years, I began to realize that the forty-six verses of Titus laid an incredible foundation for manhood. Almost every basic question a man asks on his journey to becoming a godly man was answered in this little book. And year after year, ten men at a time, I began to see God use the book of Titus to raise up a generation of godly men who were not only committed to the Lord, but committed to the church and to each other. Over time, every man in our church wanted to be a part of the Titus Ten.

When the Lord called me away from that church after eleven years, they had a reception for my family. The most surprising thing for me that evening was the number of men who came up to me, wrapped their arms around me, and with tears in their eyes told me how much Titus Ten meant to them.

The book of Titus was not specifically written to be a manual for manhood. It was written to be a manual for the local church. As one of the three pastoral epistles (1 Timothy, 2 Timothy, and Titus), it was written to clarify how the local church should best function to develop the people of God and fulfill the mission of God. There may be no more practical, concise, and comprehensive guide for the local church than the forty-six verses of Titus. But, after walking hundreds of men through Titus, I am more confident than ever this book can and should also be used as a foundation for building godly men. This becomes even more clear as we get to know Titus, the man and this letter written to him.

Titus: The Man

When Andrea and I were dating, I went to her family's home for Easter lunch. Her father made sure I sat directly to his right at the table. At some point during the meal, he turned to me and asked, in front of the whole family, one simple question. "Josh, what Bible character do you identify with the most?"

Now, my father-in-law is one of the most faithful, godly, and fun men I have ever known. He is also the most strategic and intentional man I have ever known. When he asked this question, I knew he was trying to figure out something about me.

I remember not knowing how to answer his question. I'm not sure I had ever thought about it before. I mean, certainly, I wanted to be like Jesus. But I couldn't say "Jesus." I was still trying to walk that balance between being nice and not looking like I was trying too hard. Saying "Jesus" seemed like it would have crossed that line.

I don't remember what Bible character I named, but I do remember the moment. And to this day, that simple question has continued to play a significant role in my life and ministry.

Over the years I have discovered that for a man to discern his calling, gifting, and purpose in life, that question is one he needs to answer. Finding a Bible character you identify with can bring clarity and perspective to your life. It can move you a long way down the road of understanding your own passions and gifting. My own answer to that question has given me clarity on who it is God has called me to be and what He has uniquely gifted me to do.

I have been asking men that question for fifteen years now, and over all of those years, not one man has ever said Titus. And that's a shame, because Titus was a great man, worthy of imitation.

One of the reasons no one lists Titus as their favorite Bible character might be because he's not easy to get to know. You have to dig. There are only thirteen references to him in the New Testament, and there is more we don't know than we do. We do not know when he became a follower of Jesus, when he first met Paul and began to travel with him, or anything about his personal life and family. We have no record of anything that Titus ever wrote or said. But, as we look at all the references that we have, we can piece together a picture of a man whom we would all be well served to know and imitate.

First, Titus was a faithful follower of Jesus. In Titus 1:4 (NIV) Paul refers to Titus as "my true son in a common faith." This is the same way Paul refers to Timothy (1 Tim. 1:2). Paul brought Titus on an important mission. In Acts 15 the early church was in a debate over the belief that all Gentile believers needed to be circumcised. Paul, who had been ministering to the Gentiles and strongly disagreed that all of these new converts had to be circumcised, went to Jerusalem as the apostles debated the issue. To prove that circumcision was not necessary for salvation, he brought with him a living example—an example of an uncircumcised Gentile who was so clearly a believer that his life would show how unnecessary circumcision was for the Christian. Paul brought Titus (Gal. 2:1).

Second, Titus was a courageous servant. In Acts 18 we learn that Paul spent a year and a half in Corinth with the church he had just planted. He then left there and spent two and a half years in Ephesus. Titus was most likely with him during this time. While in Ephesus, Paul received a report of how things were going at the young church in Corinth (1 Cor. 1:11). It wasn't good. So, Paul sent Timothy to check things out. Timothy soon learned that the situation was worse than Paul thought. Paul then made an urgent visit to confront the false teachers and deal with the sin in Corinth. After leaving them, he sent them a painful letter (2 Cor. 2:1–4). This letter was hard for him to write and hard for them to read. He sent that letter by the hands of Titus.

At some point, most likely while Paul was under arrest and being taken to Rome, he and Titus stopped in Crete. While there, Paul saw the false doctrine, rebellious men, and lazy gluttons present in the church. It was a church that needed godly men, sound doctrine, and courageous leadership. Paul left Titus there to put things in order (Titus 1:5).

Proverbs 25:13 says, "Like the cold of snow in the time of harvest is a faithful messenger to those who send him; he refreshes the soul of his masters." Paul felt this way about Titus. He knew that delivering this letter, waiting for them to read it, and then being able to respond to it, would not be an easy task. It demanded courage and faithfulness. This is why Paul also sent Titus to take up an offering for the church in Jerusalem (2 Cor. 8:6). Paul viewed Titus as a courageous servant, ready for the most difficult assignments. From the Jerusalem council to the church in Crete, Paul had incredible confidence in Titus, who became his go-to man for the most difficult tasks.

Finally, Titus was a beloved friend. After Titus's trip to Corinth, he was supposed to meet Paul in Troas, but he was delayed. They had a plan, knowing there was no way for them to communicate along the way. But something happened, and Titus didn't show up. Paul tells us he was in great distress when Titus never made it to Troas (2 Cor. 2:13). Paul went on to Macedonia where he was harassed at every turn and experienced conflicts all around him and fear inside of him. But, when he was downcast, he was deeply encouraged and comforted by the arrival of Titus (2 Cor. 7:6).

As I walked through Scripture trying to trace the life of Titus, Paul's deep affection for him was the most moving part of his story. To Paul, Titus was more than just a fellow worker, and courageous helper in the ministry (2 Cor. 8:23). Titus was a friend. And Paul needed a friend. Paul had been betrayed by many, but Titus remained a faithful companion.

I think the reason this part of the story resonates so much is that all of us need a friend like that. We need a friend who sticks closer than a brother. I remember the moment early in my marriage when I discovered that Andrea and I both needed friends. This was hard for me to admit. I had just assumed that once we got married, I was going to be all that Andrea needed. I assumed that as promised, I would be the fulfillment of every dream and every desire that she had. Why would she ever need anyone other than me? But the reality was, Andrea needed friends. And so did I. We all do.

The journey toward manhood demands friends. There is more and more research being done on the devastating effects of loneliness and isolation. A recent study showed that loneliness is just as lethal as smoking fifteen cigarettes a day! Lonely people are 50 percent more likely to die prematurely than those with healthy relationships. A lack of good relationships is associated with a 29-percent increase in the risk of coronary disease and 32-percent risk of stroke.[1] Doctors and scientists are just catching up with what the Bible has always told us. Isolation is physically, mentally, and spiritually dangerous (Prov. 18:1).

The temptation to remain isolated is even greater for a man. Not because men prefer isolation, but because the older we get and busier we get, the harder it is to find time to cultivate friendships. And, moving from casual acquaintance to meaningful friendship is often awkward. We tend to be satisfied with surface friendships that lack any real depth. But Paul and Titus remind us that good friendships are essential in our journey to manhood.

Titus: The Letter

Paul left Titus in Crete (Titus 1:5) to invest in a struggling church and deal with rebellious men. It's unclear whether

Titus knew just how dysfunctional this church was when Paul left him there, but this little letter seems to indicate that Paul did know. Paul knew that this church needed Titus. And he knew that Titus was uniquely gifted to help this church become healthy.

One of the primary issues infecting the church was that the pagan culture of Crete had infiltrated the culture of the church. Crete is an island in the Mediterranean off the coast of Greece. It is one of the largest islands in the Mediterranean Sea and in Paul's day was an important commercial weigh station for the seagoing trade. Because of its location, it would have been a melting pot of all kinds of religious and philosophical views. Although Olympus claimed to be the "seat of the gods," the Cretans believed those very gods were but men and women of Crete elevated to deity by their goodwill. They were not only pagan; they were proud of it.

One of the most humorous verses in the entire New Testament is found in Titus 1:12. Paul, quoting a Cretan poet, says, "Cretans are always liars, evil beasts, lazy gluttons." This is one of those moments in which you can say these kinds of harsh things about people as long as you are quoting someone saying it about himself! But Paul goes beyond that. He then says, "This testimony is true." "Yes," Paul says, "I agree with the Cretans' admission; *they are* always liars, evil beasts, and lazy gluttons!" I assume you could say these kinds of things more easily before social media. But Paul's point was that the reputation was true, and this character problem had infiltrated the church.

We do not know when the gospel was first brought to Crete. We do know there were people from Crete who heard the gospel in their language at Pentecost (Acts 2:11). Most likely, devout Jews had come from Crete to Jerusalem for Pentecost, heard the gospel, and went back to Crete to plant a church. When Paul and Titus stopped in Crete on their way to Rome, they discovered this little church.

A little and highly dysfunctional church.

There are three primary themes that Paul emphasizes to Titus to help him shepherd this church. First, Paul emphasizes the *centrality of the local church in the mission of God.* The primary concern for Paul when writing Titus is that the church at Crete would become healthy and strong to be effective in advancing Christ's kingdom. Although many things are discussed, the ultimate purpose of preparing a church to reach unbelievers effectively must not be lost. Paul desired the church both to think correctly and act correctly and to be people of both proper doctrine and proper duty.

Second, Paul wrote this book to emphasize the *centrality of the gospel in everything.* The entire book of Titus was written to combat a false understanding of the gospel. Some false teachers were adding to the gospel, and as a result, were undermining the message and ministry of the church. The church *must* get the gospel right. If not, everyone will suffer (Titus 1:11).

The book of Titus gives us two of the greatest gospel texts in all of the New Testament.

> For the grace of God has appeared, bringing salvation for all people, training us to renounce ungodliness and worldly passions, and to live self-controlled, upright, and godly lives in the present age, waiting for our blessed hope, the appearing of the glory of our great God and Savior Jesus Christ, who gave himself for us to redeem us from all lawlessness and to purify for himself a people for his possession who are zealous for good works. (Titus 2:11–14)

> But when the goodness and loving kindness of God our Savior appeared, he saved us, not because of works done by us in righteousness, but according to his mercy, by the washing of regeneration and renewal of the Holy Spirit, whom he poured out on us richly through Jesus Christ our Savior, so that being justified by his grace we might become heirs according to the hope of eternal life. (Titus 3:4–7)

And finally, Paul wrote to emphasize the *centrality of good works in the life of the believer*. The book of Titus is all about the connection between doctrine and duty, principle and practice, faith and works. Paul knew that for the people of God to reach the lost they must be a people who both think correctly and live correctly. This is why there is so much emphasis on "good works." No place in the New Testament emphasizes good deeds more strongly than Titus. Paul mentions it six times in just these few chapters (1:16; 2:7; 2:14; 3:1; 3:8; 3:14). This letter is about doing. Paul applies this instruction to the three primary areas of our lives: our church, our families, and our culture.

> God has saved us so that we might join with the local church to declare and display the gospel of Jesus Christ.

The primary message of Titus is this: God has saved us so that we might join with the local church to declare and display the gospel of Jesus Christ.

Titus: Foundations for Becoming a Godly Man

If this is essentially a manual for building a foundation in the local church, how can this also be a manual for how to lay a foundation in your life as a man? There are two compelling reasons.

First, Paul's instructed Titus to find godly men and put them into leadership. In Titus 1:5 (CSB), Paul says, "The reason

I left you in Crete was to set right what was left undone and, as I directed you, to appoint elders in every town." When it came to dealing with all of the difficulties, divisions, and false doctrine in the church, Paul wanted to make sure that first things came first.

The *first* thing that Paul instructs Titus to do is to put godly leadership in place. Before the false teaching, the immorality, and the immaturity could be fixed, there needed to be godly men in leadership. Then, Paul instructs Titus on how to find these men and what these men should be doing. The local church, as well as the family and society in general, will go the direction of the men.

Second, the book of Titus was written by one courageous godly man to another courageous godly man. It wasn't written directly to the church; it was written directly to another man. And even though 1 and 2 Timothy are also written from one man to another, those letters feel more like a father writing to a son. The book of Titus feels like Paul writing to his coworker and companion. It feels different. Paul speaks more directly to Titus. Within the forty-six verses, we start to get a clear picture of both of these men. In their words, we find a great picture of manhood.

Emerging from the pages of this little letter are ten foundations for becoming a godly man:

1. Dominion
2. Gospel

How to Read This Book

The Titus Ten does not contain everything a man needs to know. *The Titus Ten* contains ten foundations upon which a man must build a godly life. We not only need these foundations in our own life; we need these foundations as we seek to raise up a new generation of godly men.

Before you begin this journey, I want to tell you how to get the most out of it.

First, you need to read this book in the context of relationships. I want to plead with you not to read it alone. This book came to life in the context of a series of early morning men's Bible studies. I watched these foundational truths from Titus radically change men. But it did so in the context of multi-generational groups of men, sharing the Word, sharing their stories, and sharing their hearts. Ideally, you would gather men for ten weeks to walk through *The Titus Ten* together.

One of the reasons men do not often cultivate meaningful friendships is because they just don't know where to start. You don't want to just ask a guy if he would be your friend. This book is a great way to start. If you ask a few men to walk through this book with you, it gives you not only a context in which to build friendships, but also a shared experience.

Second, read this book with a commitment to action. Every chapter is written not just to inform, but to activate. The goal of this book is to raise up a generation of godly men in the church. Men of action. Men of depth. Men of courage. Solid men who have built their lives on a strong foundation. The truths contained in this book will challenge you. They will call you into being the man God wants you to be. Take the time at the end of each chapter to discuss with others the ways in which you can practically apply these things every week.

Don't allow yourself to be overwhelmed by how far you have to go. Take one step of action with every chapter. The most important thing for you to do is always the next thing God tells you to do. As the Spirit prompts you to respond, respond. Be a man of obedient action.

Finally, read this book with your eyes on Jesus. It is critical to remember that our pursuit of becoming a man is really a pursuit of a Man—the man Jesus Christ. We must discipline ourselves for the purpose of godliness (1 Tim. 4:7–8). We must apply great effort to the cultivation of godly character and virtues (2 Pet. 1:5). We must be committed to continual and strenuous effort toward the calling God has placed on our life as a man and a Christian (Phil. 2:12–13). Becoming a godly man takes time, thought, attention, effort, and action.

Yet, what we really want is not just to cultivate manly qualities, but to be conformed into the image of Jesus Christ. Jesus is the man we want to become. Jesus is the Second Adam who fulfilled God's vision for manhood. And He is not just the model of manhood; He is our only hope for becoming the man God wants us to become.

So, as you read these pages and take this journey with others, keep your eyes constantly on Jesus. Make Him your greatest pursuit. Continually invite Him into this process. Allow desire, ambition, insecurity, and deficiency to drive you to Jesus. Let's run together toward manhood with our eyes fixed on Jesus (Heb. 12:1–2). Let's begin laying a foundation for becoming a godly man.

Discussion Questions

1. How have you seen the men of the church impact the church, both negatively and positively?

2. In what ways do you see the need for strong faithful men in the church? What kind of men are lacking? What kind are needed?

3. What do you see as the primary challenges in our culture that are keeping men from being the kind of men the church needs? In other words, what in our culture is working against us as men?

4. This week, think about what Bible character you identify with or want to be like. And no, you cannot say "Jesus." If you already know who it is, share it at the table. If not, come back next week ready to share it.

Chapter 1

DOMINION

WHEN MY FAMILY and I moved to Georgia in 2017, we bought a home that sits on a little over two acres of land. To my family, who spent the previous eleven years in zero-lot homes in the suburbs of Dallas, Texas, this new home made us feel like we had become homesteaders—especially to me and my young son, as we quickly discovered the joy of exploring and working in the woods behind our house. Every chance we get, Josiah and I go into the backyard to cut down trees and dig holes just for the fun of it. To this day, I often come home from work and my son says, "Dad, let's go dig!"

Normally, as Josiah and I head out the door to work in the yard, I jokingly tell my wife we are going to take dominion over the land. Just saying those words makes me feel manly. When I walk outside, get right in the middle of the thorns and debris, and begin to clear the land and kill the weeds, I feel like I'm doing something I was created to do. And that's because, in reality, that *is* something I was created to do. Every man was. Not just in the backyard, but in every area of his life. Every man was created by God to take dominion.

Distortion vs. Intention

My favorite passage of Scripture to use at a wedding is Matthew 19:1–12. In most Bibles, the title of that passage reads, "Teaching about Divorce." That might seem like an odd choice for a wedding sermon, but in this passage, Jesus reveals God's original intention for marriage.

The religious leaders, testing Jesus, asked Him about divorce. Jesus answers by taking them back to Genesis 1–2. Why? Because, while the Pharisees wanted to talk about the distortion of marriage, Jesus wanted them to see beyond the distortion, to God's original intention.

Many people, like the religious leaders in Matthew 19, like to focus more on modern distortions, which often gets more "Amens." *Especially* when it comes to manhood.

> Calling out modern men for their failures has become a sport.

Calling out modern men for their failures has become a sport. And although there is certainly a lot to say on the distortions of manhood, the Bible takes a different approach. The Bible does not just point to modern distortions; it helps us discover original intentions.

In *The Masculine Mandate*, Richard Phillips takes us to God's original intentions for manhood in Genesis 2 and points out four essential truths about a man: who a man is, where a man is, what a man is, and how a man is to fulfill his calling. In other words, almost everything we need to know about manhood has been clearly articulated in *one* chapter of the Bible. All of God's intentions are there.

Starting in Genesis 3, the rest of the Bible shows just how spectacularly mankind can distort God's original intention. And because we see the distortions on every other page of the Bible, and in every man around us, we tend to focus more on the distortions than the intentions. But our goal is not to tear men down; it is to build them up. We are trying to lay a foundation on which to build a godly life, and we must begin with God's original intentions. That starts with dominion.

Dominion

Mankind was created to have a relationship with God, to live under God's authority, and to have authority over everything God created (Psalm 8). Adam found his true identity in his relationship with God, and he was to fulfill his God-given assignment by ruling over God's new creation on God's behalf.

In so doing, God's glory would spread to the ends of the earth (Gen. 2:10–17; Hab. 2:14).

The responsibility that God gave to Adam and Eve was clear: "Be fruitful and multiply and fill the earth and subdue it, and have dominion over the fish of the sea and the birds of the heavens and over every living thing that moves on the earth" (Gen. 1:28). To take dominion meant to take responsibility, to care, to lead, to cultivate.

And yes, God tells Adam and Eve *both* to take dominion. They both bring different and essential skills to the assignment. God's instruction to Adam and Eve shows us that God created both Adam and Eve equal in essence but distinct in roles.

> God's instruction to Adam and Eve shows us that God created both Adam and Eve equal in essence but distinct in roles.

Adam needed Eve. God was the one who looked at Adam and knew that something was missing. He could not fulfill his God-given assignment without her. Yet, God gave Adam the primary responsibility of leadership. They would work together to take dominion under Adam's direction and leadership. This is why, after Adam and Eve sinned, God called Adam and held him accountable for Eve's actions (Gen. 3:8–9).

When we read about God's original intention in Genesis 2, we get the picture of Adam leading Eve on an exhilarating adventure through life. Adam has been given this vast and beautiful domain of the earth, and he is working and tending and exploring it all. And by his side is Eve, an indispensable and irreplaceable lover and helper who finds her greatest joy in following Adam on this great adventure and helping him every step of the way. No conflict. No tension. No pride. No battle of the wills. Adam and Eve were both happy and fulfilled. They knew that they were equal. They knew their roles. They were a team. And they thrived.

The Way of Dominion

Although deeply distorted by sin, the original mandate for men to take dominion is still a mandate. It is a part of God's original intention. Everything we are trying to do, by the power of the gospel of Jesus Christ, is to get back to God's original intention for our lives. God has created men, under His authority, on His behalf, as His representatives, manifesting His character, to take dominion.

There are two words in Genesis 2 that give clarity on the meaning of dominion: *work* and *keep* (Gen. 2:15). The primary role of every man, in every area of his life, is summarized in those two words.

When you think about "work," think about a plow. A plow is used to cultivate the earth. It is used to turn up the soil and prepare the ground for seed. You can think of a hand-held instrument like a hoe, a large metal mold-board pulled behind an animal, or a 400-horse power, 8-Series John Deere tractor. Either way, the idea is to cultivate the earth so that what is planted will grow.

Plowing is a selfless and thankless task. It's hard work. It's sweaty work (unless you get that 8-Series John Deere with leather seats, cup holders, ventilated massaging seats, six-ways speakers, and XM radio). Yet, plowing is the work to which every man should be devoted. Not to tend a garden, but to sacrificially work hard for the sake of others. To sweat and toil, to cultivate and nurture everything and everyone God has put under his charge. As a man, you were created to work this way.

Every man should wake up every morning and imagine a plow in his hand and be ready to work. This is God's calling. And under your leadership, things should grow and thrive.

When you think about "keeping," think about a sword. To keep is to watch, guard, and protect. That which God has put under your charge should not only grow and thrive; it should be cared for and protected. God has created every man to be a guardian, a protector, a defender. He is called not only to stand in the watchtower and watch but to take up his sword and fight.

I have four daughters and one son. My son came last. After having four daughters, one thing my wife and I were not prepared for was the innate aggression in this little man. It was not just aggression toward his four older sisters (but to be fair, having four sisters has to be a challenge for the little guy); it became a bit of a problem in preschool too. It's always fun to start a phone conversation with the words, "This is Josh Smith, the pastor at Prince. My son is the one who put your son in a headlock on the playground earlier this week."

At one point, we went to meet with Josiah's teacher about it. She said that she had been watching him carefully and had noticed something about his aggression. She noticed that he was only aggressive when he perceived an injustice. If he saw someone being mean or felt as if someone were not doing something they should, he just took matters into his own hands and whacked them!

There is a part of his aggression that we, as his parents, need to control and discipline. You can't go through life hitting people. On the other hand, part of this needs to be cultivated instead of squelched. In reality, a lot of it is just the man in him. God has created him to carry a sword. God has put inside of his little heart a desire to defend. To protect those around him. It is a desire to keep.

This desire and this calling have been placed in every man. It is in you. Someone might have taken the sword from your hand and sin might have distorted the way you use it, but you were created to carry a sword. You were created to defend and protect. You were created to stand against injustice and sacrificially lay down your life for the good of those around you.

Working and keeping are at the very core of manhood. God models both for us in the garden. He creates us in His image so we might reflect His glory by doing the same. When you work and keep, as a man living under the authority of Jesus Christ and filled with the Holy Spirit, you bear the image of God and begin to lay a foundation for manhood.[2]

Domains

The areas in which God calls a man to take dominion are called domains. You can't give a man dominion without giving him a domain. God created Adam to take dominion and then gave him a domain in which to work: "The LORD God took the man and put him in the garden of Eden to work it and keep it" (Gen. 2:15). The domain in which Adam was to wield his plow and his sword was in the garden. The garden was his responsibility.

We will talk more specifically about dominion within domains in the chapter on assignments, but to lay a foundation for manhood, we must understand in broad terms the primary domains that God has given every single man.

This is where the structure of the book of Titus is helpful for us. John Stott, in his commentary of Titus, says that Titus can easily be divided up into the three primary areas of Christian living: the church, the home, and the world. Many other commentators have noticed the same divisions.

Titus 1 focuses almost entirely on the church itself and the need for men to lead in the church. Titus 2 focuses on the people of the church and how both men and women should live. Titus 3 focuses on what it means to live as a Christian outside the church in the world and more specifically in the workplace.

The church, the home, and the workplace are the three primary domains of every man. But for a man to take dominion in those areas, he must first take dominion in another area, an area that is seen in every chapter of Titus. *A man must first take dominion over his flesh.*

> These four areas—the flesh, church, family, and work—are every man's four primary domains.

These four areas—the flesh, church, family, and work—are every man's four primary domains. I also believe the order of these domains is the priority of every man.

Domain 1: Flesh

A few years ago, as I was looking to add some new staff members at our church, I reached out to an older pastor and mentor and asked for some advice. Specifically, I wanted to know what questions he asked in the interview process. He told me he always asks a man to give a "personal overcomer story"—a story of overcoming some area of sin or temptation in his own life. And then this pastor said, "If a man has not learned how to control his flesh and get personal victory over sin, he has no business being a pastor."

He's right. And it's not just about being a pastor. Our ability to take dominion over our flesh will directly determine our ability to take dominion in every area of our life. The first battle in every man's life is the battle with his sinful nature. If we lose that one, we can't win any other one.

After Paul tells Titus to find good men and put them in leadership, he tells Titus what to look for. Listen to how he describes the men the church needs:

> If anyone is above reproach, the husband of one wife, and his children are believers and not open to the charge of debauchery or insubordination. For an overseer, as God's steward, must be above reproach. He must not be arrogant or quick-tempered or a drunkard or violent or greedy for gain, but hospitable, a lover of good, self-controlled, upright, holy,

and disciplined. He must hold firm to the
trustworthy word as taught, so that he may
be able to give instruction in sound doctrine
and also to rebuke those who contradict it.
(Titus 1:6–9)

Apart from the direct reference to a man having self-
control, there are multiple references to things that demand
self-control. A man must be able to control his pride, his
temper, his drinking, and his flesh. A man cannot be a leader
until he learns to take dominion over himself.

This is why Paul said, "I discipline my body and keep it
under control, lest after preaching to others I myself should be
disqualified" (1 Cor. 9:27). Paul was very aware that after a
lifetime of gospel preaching he could be completely disqualified if he did not take dominion over his flesh. I don't need
to illustrate this. You have seen countless men undermine a
lifetime of good with a momentary failure to control the lust
of the flesh.

We often talk about men having a "moral fall." We say
"moral fall" as if to say that a man was doing great, walking
with Jesus, fighting sin, overcoming his flesh, when all of
a sudden, out of nowhere, he fell into sin. This is never the
case. Men do not have quick moral falls; they have slow moral
slides. Behind every moral fall is years of failure to control the
flesh.

Taking dominion over your flesh is not just about fighting against sin. We will never gain any victory over sin unless we truly believe that walking with Jesus is better than living in sin. We should long for the life, joy, peace, and blessing that come when we walk with Jesus. Our primary motive is always more of Jesus.

This will be a theme throughout this book: the foundation of our lives will always crumble if we do not begin with working and keeping our flesh. No matter what else you build, the foundation of self-control must be laid. If it is not, the building will ultimately fall.

Domain 2: Church

What I am going to say right now might seem completely foreign, and even wrong to many of you, but I am convinced it is true. Before your family or your work, your greatest areas of sacrificial and loving leadership should be in the local church to which you have committed yourself. This is where you learn to use your plow and sword in the home and workplace.

Paul was writing Titus to help him fix a church in turmoil (Titus 1:5). The primary cause of turmoil was the presence of useless, ungodly, and rebellious men (1:10–16). The first thing Paul tells Titus to do is find godly men (men who have cultivated self-control) and put them in leadership in the church. The first place he calls godly men into action is the church.

The church is the body of Christ. The church is the bride of Christ. The church is the house of God. The church is the family of God. God uses those metaphors so we might understand His love for the church. And "church" is not just a reference to all believers, but to local assemblies in which the body, bride, house, and family are manifested.

You cannot say you love Christ if you do not love His bride. You cannot say you are serving Christ if you are not an active part of His body. If you are not sacrificially attending, serving, and supporting a local church, you cannot become the man God wants you to be. God has set His church as the primary place in which He works in and through men. You cannot expect God to bless your life if you reject His means of doing so! And, if you are unwilling to commit yourself to a church, you are undermining all the good work God wants to do in you.

> If you are not sacrificially attending, serving, and supporting a local church, you cannot become the man God wants you to be.

The local church is not only the primary place in which a man learns to be a Christian; it is the primary place in which a man learns to be a man. It is there, surrounded by generations of godly men, that he learns about himself and his God. Find a church and make it a priority. Give it your greatest effort. Serve it, love it, and protect it. Work and keep it.

Domain 3: Family

Your next domain is your family. If you are young and/or single, don't skip this section. This also includes you.

The reason marriage comes after the church is that the family exists to point to the relationship between Christ and His church. The church is the greater of the two. But these things do not conflict; they both thrive when they are given their proper place in a man's life. A healthy church is made up of healthy families.

One of the reasons a young man must learn to take dominion over his flesh and then must learn how to sacrificially love and lead in the church is because both of those things prepare him to take dominion in the home. I want you to think about this. When a father allows his family to make other things more important than the church, the father undermines the primary training ground for his family. God has given us the local church as the means to train us in how to love those in our family (this is the point of Titus 2).

One of the most important pieces of advice I give to husbands regularly is simply this: go home and work. God has entrusted you with that family. It is your domain. It is your responsibility. It demands the constant use of the plow and the sword. Serve your wife. Serve your children. Be the hardest worker at home. Give yourself sacrificially every single day for the good of your family. And it's not just about working hard and providing. It's about doing the hard work of loving and leading and helping at home. A woman will not despise the idea of godly dominion if she sees this manifested in the way you love, serve, and help at home.

This is not just for husbands and fathers. I had a middle school boy ask me recently, "Why is it so hard to be nice to my mom?" I loved the honesty of that question. I think most middle school boys, if they were honest, would ask the same question. My answer was simple. God is teaching you how to be a man by teaching you how to love, serve, and respect your mom, even when you don't feel like it. The home is the training ground for godly, sacrificial, servant-hearted dominion. And learning to take dominion as a young man, looks like working and keeping in your home in a way that honors Jesus.

Domain 4: Work

Finally, we take dominion in the workplace. Titus transitions from life in the church (chapter 1) to life in the home (chapter 2), to life in the workplace (chapter 3). Titus 3 begins with these words to employees: "Remind them to be submissive to rulers and authorities, to obey, to be ready for every good work, to slander no one, to avoid fighting, and to be kind, always showing gentleness to all people." Notice that to be a godly man at work, you must learn through the ministry of the local church and the ministry in the home how to obey, work, deal with conflict, and be kind.

Part of using your plow and sword in the workplace means working hard and providing for those under your care. Without question, every husband has been given the primary role of financial provision. First Timothy 5:8 says that a man who does not provide for his family is worse than an unbeliever. Every man should carry the primary weight for financial provision. But a man's responsibility in the workplace does not end with provision.

The workplace is where a man displays to a lost world what self-sacrificing, loving, and godly dominion looks like. It is where a man shows the world God's original intention. Paul says, "Whatever you do, work heartily, as for the Lord and not for men" (Col. 3:23). No one should be a harder worker, a better employee, or a better boss than a man who follows Jesus. You should work harder, sacrifice more, and lead more graciously than anyone else. In so doing, you are not only seeking your good and the good of those under your charge; you are seeking to glorify God through your work ethic.

> No one should be a harder worker, a better employee, or a better boss than a man who follows Jesus.

The Wisdom of God in Domains

Do you see the wisdom of God in our domains? Do you see the wisdom of God in the order of our domains? At a young age, a man should be learning how to control his flesh. And in the local church, he is seeing how to love and serve and give of himself sacrificially for the good of others. And then in the home, he is applying what he sees in the church and learns how to work hard, love well, be kind, and be submissive to authority. Then, from his dominion in those three areas, he learns how to be a successful man in the workplace. God knows what He is doing when He clarifies those domains and tells us the proper order.

Have you ever known a man who just couldn't keep a job? In my experience, as I have talked with these men, I have noticed there is almost always a reason why he can't keep a job. And sadly, everyone sees it but the man himself. While he blames everyone else for his misfortune, everyone else knows he's the one to blame. In most of these cases, the problem goes back to this man's failure to learn in his own life, in the church, and in the home, how to take godly, loving, sacrificial dominion. He does not know how to work and keep. He does not pick up his plow and sword. And as a result, he is often—like many of the men in Crete—"unfit for any good work" (Titus 1:16).

The only reason the world has a problem with the idea of manly dominion is that they have not seen dominion as God intended it. To use your plow and sword in your domains is to work hard, sweat, toil, and sacrifice for the good of those under your charge. It is about manifesting the very death of Christ for the good of others. Taking dominion is about displaying the gospel. It's about seeing the way sin has distorted God's original intention. It is about manifesting the glory of God. It is about God's original intention. It is about having our manhood redeemed. And that is where we go next.

Discussion Questions

1. How does the idea of dominion resonate with you? Do you sense that God has created you to work and keep?

2. What are the negative effects of men not taking dominion in our day? How are people suffering by the lack of godly dominion? Think about it in all four primary areas: flesh, church, family, and work.

3. Personally, in which of the four areas do you find it most difficult to walk in dominion? Why?

4. In what area do you feel like you need to be walking in more dominion right now? Be specific.

Chapter 2

GOSPEL

DONALD RUMSFELD, FORMER United States Secretary of Defense, said, "If you drop a pebble in a pond, the ripples go out. . . . The test is, how big a stone can you throw in the pond?"[3]

Every action we take, whether big or small, positive or negative, has a rippling effect. Every decision, every word, every step, every moment will have some influence on your life and the lives of others.

Many years before reading that quote by Donald Rumsfeld, I learned about these rippling effects from the moral failure of my grandfather. His decision to leave his wife broke my grandmother's heart. It was the impetus to her early-onset dementia and premature death. For years after his decision, his four grown children, one of whom is my mom, wrestled with the hurt, anger, embarrassment, and bitterness brought on by their father's surprising actions. His grandchildren spent years trying to process the failure of the man they saw as the family's

deeply rooted and unwavering oak tree. Although my grandfather eventually repented of his sin, he lived the rest of his life
with regrets and shame. *Oh, the rippling effects of one decision.*

There is no place that we see the rippling effects of one
decision more than in the garden of Eden. In one moment,
Adam and Eve believed the lie of the enemy. They believed
that there was something better than life with God. And with
one decision, as Adam and Eve rebelled against a holy God
and sin entered into the world, everything was broken.

Brokenness is not the same as sin. Sin is rebellion against
a holy God. Brokenness is the effect of that rebellion in our
lives and the world around us. When we see the brokenness in
our lives, our marriages, our relationships, our world—we are
seeing the rippling effects of sin. Sin brought brokenness into
every area of life, including our manhood.

When Paul wrote to Titus and gave him instructions on
how to navigate all the dysfunction in the church at Crete, he
told him to begin by dealing with the rebellious men. Paul
wrote, "For there are many who are insubordinate, empty talkers, and deceivers" (Titus 1:10). These men were dividing the
church, disrupting families, and destroying the church's effectiveness and witness. And most of these actions were caused by
a group Paul refers to as "the circumcision party" (1:10).

The "circumcision party" refers to a group of people who
believed and preached a false gospel. They were teaching that
to become a Christian, you not only had to accept Jesus as the

Messiah, but you must also be circumcised and follow Old Testament regulations. This false gospel, taught by these rebellious men, was tearing the church apart.

The root issue in Crete was not just the rebellious men, but a misunderstood and misapplied gospel taught by rebellious men.

If you get everything in life right but get the gospel wrong, you have nothing right. The gospel forms everything and brings clarity to everything. The gospel changes everything and is the foundation of everything. The gospel is the only way you will know how to take what is broken and put it back together. Especially manhood.

> The gospel is the only pathway out of a distorted view of manhood back to God's original intention for manhood.

The gospel is the only pathway out of a distorted view of manhood back to God's original intention for manhood.

Where Was Adam?

In the garden, Adam and Eve walked in perfect communion with God and perfect intimacy with one another. Everything inside of them and everything around them flourished. The world, and their own lives, were marked by light, love, beauty, freedom, and joy. Nothing was broken.

But in one moment, everything changed. When Eve believed the lie of the enemy and ate the forbidden fruit, she didn't just choose sin; she rejected God. Sin, at its very core, is rebellion. Sin is rebellion against God's authority over our lives and a declaration that we can rule ourselves and the world better without Him. And that lie, the lie that we can function without God, always leads to brokenness. Every single time.

We see the rippling effects of sin as brokenness immediately spreads (Gen. 3:15–19). The wages of sin is death, and something in Adam and Eve immediately died. The life they once knew was gone, and in its place were shame, pride, anger, lust, envy, and a host of other sins. Those sins became their new reality. And those sins complicated everything.

In one moment, Eve was broken, Adam was broken, marriage was broken, and all creation was broken. And ever since, we have lived in a broken world.

We all probably know the story of Eve listening to the Serpent and taking the fruit from him. But have you ever wondered, when all of this was going down, *where was Adam?* While Eve was making this monumental decision that would affect the rest of mankind for the rest of eternity, what was Adam doing?

We often have this picture in our minds of Eve walking alone when Satan tempted her. Maybe that's because most depictions we have seen, starting with the pictures in our children's Bible, show Eve all alone having a conversation with the snake. But if we read the story, we see a different picture. Look carefully. You might have missed this verse. "So when the woman saw that the tree was good for food, and that it was a delight to the eyes, and that the tree was to be desired to make one wise, she took of its fruit and ate, and she also gave some to her husband *who was with her,* and he ate" (Gen. 3:6, emphasis mine). Where was Adam? He was *with her.*

Adam was right there. Adam was not out naming animals in a distant land when Eve sinned. He was standing next to her!

Adam was there when the serpent deceived Eve. That is why, when God came looking for them, he called Adam (v. 9). He questioned Adam (v. 11). He held Adam accountable for this decision. Adam, in a spectacular display of broken manhood, immediately blamed both God and Eve for what happened (v. 12). Yet, the New Testament consistently puts the blame on Adam and refers to original sin as the sin of Adam (Rom. 5; 1 Cor. 15:21–22). And it is here, even before the moment when Eve took a bite, that we begin to see the brokenness of manhood.

Manhood Broken

Before Eve's sin, Adam had already lost the battle for both of them. God told Adam and Eve to take dominion over the earth (Gen. 1:28), a commission in which Adam was called to be the leader and Eve was called to be the indispensable helper

(2:18–25). Adam's responsibility was to "work" and "keep." God equipped Adam with a plow and a sword and called him—in a life of selfless love—to cultivate, grow, and protect everything under his charge.

But in the garden, before Eve was tempted, Adam put down his plow and sword.

While the Serpent had a conversation with Eve, deceiving her with his words, Adam stood by and did nothing. And then, he dared to blame *her* for the sin. In a sense, the original sin was not just Eve eating from the fruit, but Adam failing to care for her soul and defend her from the Serpent. And that is a crystal-clear picture of the brokenness of manhood.

At the very core, the brokenness of manhood always comes down to the plow and the sword. When a man is self-willed and not living under the rule of God, he misuses his plow and sword. This primarily happens in one of two ways: aggression or passivity. Some men pick up their plow and sword and use them aggressively to dominate and control. Other men lay down their plow and sword and passively watch as those under their care are harassed and abused. Adam did both. He passively stood there while Eve was tempted and then immediately shifted the blame to Eve in an act of self-centered aggression.

Manhood Redeemed and Restored

Brokenness can only be put together by the gospel of Jesus Christ. The gospel is not just good news for the future; the gospel is good news for today. It is not just a guide to lead us to heaven later, but a guide to lead us into life now. When we believe the good news of the gospel and choose to trust and follow Jesus, God begins to lead us out of our broken manhood.

The book of Titus reveals just how the gospel affects every area of our lives. In the forty-six verses of this little book, we have two of the most beautiful gospel passages in all of the New Testament. The placement of these passages within the book is significant.

In chapter 2, after giving practical instruction to the men and women of the church, telling them how they should live as the people of God, Paul reminds them of the gospel. Then in chapter 3, after instructing them how to live for Christ in the workplace, Paul reminds them of the gospel. Why? Because the only way we become the people God intended us to become, and live the way that God calls us to live, is by having our lives deeply rooted in the gospel. You can only

> When we believe the good news of the gospel and choose to trust and follow Jesus, God begins to lead us out of our broken manhood.

become a godly man when your life is built on the foundation of the gospel.

Look at these two gospel passages:

> For the grace of God has appeared, bringing salvation for all people, training us to renounce ungodliness and worldly passions, and to live self-controlled, upright, and godly lives in the present age, waiting for our blessed hope, the appearing of the glory of our great God and Savior Jesus Christ, who gave himself for us to redeem us from all lawlessness and to purify for himself a people for his possession who are zealous for good works. (Titus 2:11–14)

> For we ourselves were once foolish, disobedient, led astray, slaves to various passions and pleasures, passing our days in malice and envy, hated by others and hating one another. But when the goodness and loving kindness of God our Savior appeared, he saved us, not because of works done by us in righteousness, but according to his own mercy, by the washing of regeneration and renewal of the Holy Spirit, whom he poured out on us richly through Jesus Christ our Savior, so that being justified by his grace we might become heirs

according to the hope of eternal life. (Titus 3:3–7)

The amazing thing about the gospel is that a child can believe it and a theologian can never mine the depths of it. If you were to read these two passages every day for the rest of your life, you would find something new every day. At the same time, these passages give us a basic understanding of the gospel and its implications for our lives. These verses show us the path to a restored and redeemed manhood. They also show us four gospel truths on which we must build our life.

The Gospel

First, sin has enslaved you. You are a broken person. Deeply and painfully broken. Every man is. No exceptions.

All of us were once foolish, disobedient, deceived, and enslaved (3:3). At your very core, having been born in sin and under the bondage of the enemy (Eph. 2:1–3), you are deeply broken. No one should have to convince you of this. Deep in your heart, you know that something is broken.

No man can become a godly man unless he first admits that he is a godless man. As Ephesians 2 reminds us, we were born spiritually dead, disobedient, and doomed. And we are, by our very nature, children of wrath (Eph. 2:1–3). We were born slaves to sin, living under the dominion of darkness, and completely unable to save ourselves (Col. 1:13). Without

Christ, every attempt we make to be better will ultimately fall short. We don't just need external change; we need internal change. Because our biggest problem is a sin problem.

Somewhere, early in my Christian life, I learned a very important lesson about sin. I don't know if I read it in a book or heard it in a sermon, but I know it had a significant impact on my life. I learned there is great hope in seeing sin as your greatest problem. You see, if my problem is sociological, psychological, or mental, I may or may never have a solution. But if my primary problem is sin, there is always a solution. Seeing my brokenness as sin actually gives me hope!

> There is great hope in seeing sin as your greatest problem.

Second, God is pursuing you. We have a God who is good, loving, kind, and gracious (Titus 3:4). Yes, as those who have rebelled against God and rejected Him, we are under the righteous wrath of God. We deserve eternal hell. But as God's creation, we are cared for by God. He wants to see us saved and restored, and He is pursuing us to that end. The reason this is such good news is that none of us would pursue God if left to ourselves (Rom. 3:10–17). Any desire you have for God is because God is pursuing you.

Right now, while reading this book, if you feel some desire for God and godliness, that means God is working in your life.

What an encouraging thought. God is calling you to Himself. He is inviting you to come to Him. Every desire for God is an invitation from God.

Third, Jesus came to redeem you. God displays His grace and pursuit through the appearance of Jesus Christ. Jesus has come to bring salvation to all people (Titus 2:11). And Jesus saves us by redeeming us from all lawlessness (v. 14). To "redeem" means to release a captive, like a prisoner or a slave, through the payment of ransom. Jesus came to purchase us, with His very blood, and free us from the bondage of sin. He released us by purchasing us with His blood. That is what this text tells us—He gave Himself *for us*—so that we might be released. His ransom was our redemption. Through Christ, we can not only be saved from sin but saved from the just wrath of God.

This is massively good news. Our primary issue is not brokenness; our primary issue is sin. All of the brokenness in our lives is a result of sin. If you try to fix the broken parts of your life but don't find a cure for your sin, you will never get out of your brokenness.

Men try this all the time. You don't need self-help. You need divine help. The only way into restored manhood is by having your sin taken care of. Through redemption, Jesus has purchased you, released you from slavery, and brought you to Himself. He has made it possible for you to have your manhood restored. But the only way for that to happen is through trusting the work that Jesus has done for you on the cross.

For that redemption to be applied, you must turn from your sin, turn to Jesus, trust Him to save you through His death, burial, and resurrection, and then surrender your life to Him. When you call upon the Lord and ask Him to save you, He does. He releases you from slavery and begins the process of restoring you to true manhood. But please hear this—*there is absolutely no restoration of manhood apart from a relationship with Jesus Christ.* You must choose right now to trust and follow Jesus.

> The only way into restored manhood is by having your sin taken care of.

Finally, salvation restores you. One of the most helpful parts of these two gospel passages in Titus is the reminder that Jesus did not just come merely to save you from hell; He came to put you on a path toward restoring your true identity in Him. He has saved us from sin and is "instructing us to deny godlessness and worldly lusts and to live in a sensible, righteous, and godly way in the present age" (2:12 CSB). He has redeemed you to make for Himself a people who are zealous for good deeds (v. 14). Salvation is a present-tense reality in which every day you choose to trust and follow Jesus. As you do, God takes you further down the path of restoration.

Following Jesus into True Manhood

As those who have been saved by God, how do we begin to walk that path toward the restoration of our manhood? Simply put—we follow Jesus. Jesus is called the Second Adam (1 Cor. 15). Jesus, Son of God and son of man, did what Adam did not do. He took His plow and sword and used them perfectly. He lived a life of love, humility, self-sacrifice, and service. Jesus is the model for true manhood. He is the man we long to be. He is the man God has called us to be like. He is the man those around us need us to be like. He is the man we strive to be like. And, because of the glorious news of the gospel, He is the man into whose image God is conforming us.

God saves you so He might then conform you into the image of Jesus (Rom. 8:29). This happens as we make the choice to submit ourselves daily to the lordship of Jesus, seek to be filled with the Spirit of Jesus, and strive to live out the life of Jesus. In other words, as we live out the gospel in our daily lives, our manhood is restored.

We not only believe in the rippling effects of sin, we believe in the rippling effects of Christlikeness. The man you long to be, the man God desires for you to be, the man your family needs you to be, is the man God is going to make you into, one decision at a time. And that begins with the first decision, to trust and follow Jesus Christ.

The Crowd and the Disciples

When Jesus went up to a mountain to deliver His longest recorded sermon, the Sermon on the Mount, the audience consisted of two distinct groups of people: the crowd and the disciples. Matthew 5:1–2 says, "Seeing the crowds, he went up on the mountain, and when he sat down, his disciples came to him. And he opened his mouth and taught them." There are a large crowd of people and a small group of disciples. And although the large crowd is present and listening, Jesus seems to be speaking to the smaller crowd. He is preaching to His disciples.

The "crowd" was a group of people who liked Jesus. They were fascinated by Him, intrigued by His words and actions. Wherever Jesus went, there they were. The crowd was aware of His healing powers and miraculous works, and they wanted to get in on that. They were caught up in the excitement and didn't want to miss anything. They are called "the crowd" because there were a lot of them. There always is.

And then, there are the disciples. This is a smaller group of people who don't just like being around Jesus but have decided to trust and follow Jesus. So, when Jesus sits down on a mountain to teach about the way to live life in the kingdom of God, He is speaking to those who are a part of the kingdom—His disciples. The crowd is listening, but the sermon is not for them. Instruction on living as a follower of Jesus doesn't matter too much for those who are not following Jesus.

Throughout the ministry of Jesus, we see these two groups. And to the casual observer, they look pretty much the same. But Jesus knew the difference. He knew that some of these people were just fascinated, while others were committed. He knew that some of these people just liked hearing Him, while others were following Him. Jesus knew that some were just around, while others were all-in.

Jesus was never impressed by the crowd. The crowd didn't make Him feel better about His ministry. He was never interested in building a crowd. He didn't see any real value in a large crowd of fascinated people. Jesus wanted disciples. He wanted people to trust and follow Him, not just be around Him.

So, at the end of His sermon, even though His primary audience was His disciples and He was aware the crowd was still listening, Jesus ends His sermon with an invitation:

> "Everyone then who hears these words of mine and does them will be like a wise man who built his house on the rock. And the rain fell, and the floods came, and the winds blew and beat on that house, but it did not fall, because it had been founded on the rock. And everyone who hears these words of mine and does not do them will be like a foolish man who built his house on the sand. And the rain fell, and the floods came, and the winds blew

and beat against that house, and it fell, and great was the fall of it." (Matt. 7:24–27)

This is a great invitation. It not only calls the crowd to respond; it tells them how to respond, and the consequences of not responding. Responding to Jesus means not only hearing Him, but trusting and following Him. It is believing He is the only one who can save you from your sins, the only one who has life, and the only one who knows the way to God. And then, in response to that belief, it is choosing to walk in obedience to His commands. Trust and follow.

Hearing is not enough. The crowd and the disciples heard the sermon. The crowd was even amazed by His preaching (Matt. 7:28). That's great—but the real question for the crowd was this: *Do you trust Jesus enough to follow Him? Will you build your life on Him? Will you choose to follow Him?*

And the consequences of this decision are dramatic. Those who hear Christ's words but refuse to trust and follow Him will ultimately see their lives crumble like a home without a solid foundation. But those who do trust and follow Jesus will be like a house built on a rock. When the wind blows and the storm comes, the house will not fall.

Over the past twenty years of pastoral ministry, I have discovered there are a lot of men *in the crowd*. And although it's often hard for me to discern between them and the disciples, Jesus knows the difference. And Jesus knows the dangers.

In every man's life, the storms are going to come. The winds are going to blow. Life will be filled with innumerable challenges and struggles. And the storms will ultimately expose you (Matt. 13:1–8). The crowd will crumble. The disciples will stand.

Nothing matters more in your life right now than making sure you are a disciple, not just a member of the crowd. You must have the courage to step out of the larger crowd and into the smaller group of disciples. This is the starting place of a godly life—the foundation. And now is the time. Don't settle for being around Jesus; trust and follow Him with your whole heart.

> The crowd will crumble. The disciples will stand.

Discussion Questions

1. How have you personally seen the rippling effects of sin?

2. In what ways do you most see the brokenness of manhood in your own life?

3. In what areas do you feel most deficient as a man and how can the Gospel lead you out of that? Be specific.

4. Are you confident that you are a disciple, not just a member of the crowd?

Chapter 3

IDENTITY

EARLY IN MY pastoral ministry, I asked my uncle, Tom Elliff, to preach at the church where I pastored. He preached a message on "The Curse of Words." He talked about how certain phrases in our past, most of which were not intended to be hurtful, get stuck in our minds and stay with us for a lifetime. These words can have an untold number of damaging effects on us. And everyone has them.

After he finished the message, a member of my church in his mid-seventies came up to me and asked if he could tell me a story. He told me about being raised in a very small country church where the Sunday morning music was only made up of the voices in the congregation. One Sunday, when he was just a boy, an older lady in the church told him he was singing off-key. It was a thoughtless comment that was most likely never intended to have a lingering, negative effect. But because of that one careless phrase, the man told me he had not sung in church once for more than sixty years.

The curse of words.

Death and life are in the power of the tongue, Solomon tells us (Prov. 18:21). With our tongue we can praise the Lord and curse human beings, who have been made in God's likeness, James adds (James 3:9). Words define us. And often, a casual and thoughtless word can negatively define us for years.

We have a rule in our house that no one is allowed to make any negative "you are" statements. I will often hear one of my children saying to one of their siblings, "You are so annoying." Most likely, the sibling was being annoying. But there is a difference between saying "You are acting annoying" and saying "You *are* annoying." "You are" statements define us.

Everyone has an identity. Your identity is who you think you are. Whether you realize it or not, your identity is most formed by words others have said to you, phrases that begin with words like, "You are . . . ," "You will never be . . . ," or "You are just like . . ." These careless words define us and leave many of us with an inner monologue that continues to reinforce a false identity. They really are a curse. And we all have them.

Some of you have been living under the curse of words for too long. You have little phrases that repeat in your head over and over again, like a broken record, reinforcing a false identity. And these phrases not only define you; they determine the direction of your life.

When we trust and follow Jesus, He makes us into a new creation. He redefines us. And on the pathway to a restored manhood, we must continue to allow our identity to be formed by the reality of who we are in Christ. We must hear Jesus say, "You are."

Who Are You?

Fill in the blanks: My name is _____ and I am a _____.

The first blank is easy. You have a name. You didn't choose it. It was given to you. You've had it your whole life. It's what people call you. You don't have to think about it. You don't have to hesitate when people ask you. You've said it a million times.

The second blank might be a little more difficult. There are a lot of things that could go there. My first thought when I look at that second blank is, *Where do I start?* I am a lot of things. And so are you. At times I feel like I am an overwhelming number of things, a lot of different things to a lot of different people, a lot of different things at a lot of different times. Sound familiar?

Despite the difficulty, our ability to clearly and quickly fill in that second blank is equally as important as the first one.

The first blank is just your name. The second blank is your identity. Or at least, it should be.

The reason we struggle filling in that second blank is that our first thought is most often not our identity, but our assignments. Identity and assignments are distinct but inseparable parts of every man. Identity answers the question, "Who am I?" Assignment answers the question, "What has God called me to do?" And our failure to make that distinction can lead to a lot of pain, frustration, anxiety, and a host of other issues.

I remember spending hours with James after he had lost his job during a recession. He had been successful, respected, and sought after in his field. But in a moment, it was all gone. He was surprised by how difficult it was for him. There were certainly some expected areas of pride and fear that the loss of a job exposed. But he was noticing it was deeper than that. He was having a harder time with this than he should. And he knew it. What was going on?

> Confusing your identity with your assignments can be devastating.

The loss of his job revealed he had allowed his assignment to become his identity. And when his assignment was gone, he didn't know who he was.

Confusing your identity with your assignments can be devastating. We feel the fragility of our assignments and long to base our lives on something more substantial. Thankfully, we can.

Knowing Your Identity

To build your life on a solid, unshakable foundation, you must let the gospel redefine you. So far, we have moved from intentions (created to work and keep) to distortions (sin makes everything broken). Now, we want to begin moving down the pathway toward true manhood. This begins as you not only understand and receive the gospel, but as you allow the gospel to begin to show you your true identity (2 Cor. 5:17).

The apostle Paul didn't have trouble filling in the second blank. We see this at the beginning of Titus. With five words, Paul gives his name and his identity. "Paul, a servant of God" (1:1). "Servant" is Paul's most common reference to himself (Rom. 1:1; 2 Cor. 4:5; Gal. 1:10; Phil. 1:1). This is Paul's identity. His assignment is what he says next. "Paul, a servant of God and an apostle" (we will talk about assignments in the next chapter). Paul knows who he is. And that kind of clarity is liberating and empowering.

God longs for you to clarify your identity and be able to articulate it. Your identity in Christ should make you feel like a solid man. This is why the Bible continually reminds us of who we are in Christ. We could turn to almost any book of the New Testament and find clarity on our true identity.

Take Ephesians 1, for example. In one long Greek sentence, Paul begins his letter by clarifying the true identity of all those who are "in Christ." He says that all of those who are "in Christ" are blessed, chosen, predestined, adopted, redeemed, forgiven, heirs, and homes for the Spirit of God. And that's just one sentence! There are hundreds of similar passages that clarify our identity. Yet, most men still don't know who they are.

When it comes to understanding our true manhood, and becoming godly men, four primary words must become your core identity. You are a *slave, a son, a friend,* and *a lover.*[4]

You Are a Slave

A few years ago, I was asked to be the "camp pastor" at a student camp. I would not only speak every morning but also counsel students after the evening session. One evening, the sermon was on total surrender to Jesus Christ. And although I was there to counsel those who wanted to respond to the sermon, I felt like I needed to respond.

As the preacher called the students to trust God with every area of life, surrendering complete control to Him, I felt unable to articulate those words for myself. I loved Jesus. I wanted Him to be Lord. But I found myself wrestling with God for an entire night before I could get on my knees and again submit myself, my future, my health, and my family to the Lord.

There is something about this kind of surrender that is difficult for every man. We want to be our own man; we don't want to be owned or controlled by someone else. We want to chart our course and be free. We are afraid of what it would mean to allow someone else to have control.

When Jesus invited people to Himself, He simply said, "Follow Me." Following Him demanded faith and repentance. To follow Jesus, you must believe that He alone is the way, truth, and life. Then, you must be willing to completely submit your life to Him. You must be willing to become a slave of Jesus Christ. And as counterintuitive as it seems, true manhood and true freedom begin when you choose to become a slave.

What does it mean to be a slave? "A slave is one who is in a permanent relation of servitude to another, his will being altogether consumed in the will of the other. Generally, one serving, bound to serve, in bondage."[5] There are five parallels between biblical Christianity and first-century slavery: exclusive ownership, complete submission, singular devotion, total dependence, and personal accountability.[6]

> True manhood and true freedom begin when you choose to become a slave.

Everything in our lives begins with the daily decision to allow our wills to be consumed with the will of Christ. This is the greatest battle of our lives—the battle to submit to Jesus Christ and allow Him to call the shots. You are a slave. And there is nothing more freeing than being a slave to Jesus.

For me, the struggle in completely surrendering to Jesus was fear. I was afraid of what it would mean for me, my family, and my future. I was afraid of the cost. But the Lord reminded me that perfect love casts out fear (1 John 4:18). If God loves me perfectly, I don't have to be afraid to trust Him.

You don't have to be afraid of being fully surrendered to Jesus. You don't have to be your own man. You don't have to chart your course. You don't have to figure everything out. You just have to be a faithful and submissive servant of Jesus Christ. You must surrender completely to Him.

You Are a Son

At the baptism of Jesus, God the Father opened up the heavens and declared to His Son, so that everyone there could hear, "You are my beloved Son; with you I am well pleased" (Mark 1:11). With those words, the Father gave the Son the three things every son needs most from his father: acceptance, affection, and affirmation. There will always be a void in a man's life unless he receives those three things from his father.[7]

Unfortunately, few men ever hear words like that from their earthly father. And as much as men try to act like they are okay without those things, they are not. The lack of those three things leaves a wound in the heart of every man. Although that wound can be partially healed by a healthy relationship with a man's earthly father, it can only truly be healed by a healthy relationship with our heavenly Father.

Because of your union with Christ, you are adopted into the family of God and have become a child of God. As a result, your heavenly Father says to you, "You are Mine. I love you. I'm proud of you." You find in Him the acceptance, affection, and affirmation you long for. This may sound strange, but you have to allow yourself to hear those words spoken to you. No matter what anyone else has ever said to you, if you are a child of God, God loves you and is proud of you.

I was in Mali, West Africa, the first time I was confronted with the reality of the Father's love of me. In the middle of a prayer conference, I realized for the first time that God accepts me, loves me, and is proud of me, regardless of my actions. I didn't need to work for it or earn it. It was already mine through Christ. God sees me through the lens of Jesus Christ. As a result, I am a beloved son. When I realized that, I broke down in tears.

> God loves you and is proud of you.

From that moment on I have made it my habit to always talk to men about the Father love of God. Countless times I have seen men break when they finally come to the realization that they are fully accepted and loved sons of God (Rom. 8).

When that becomes a reality in a man's life, it heals something he didn't even know was wounded.

Through faith in Jesus Christ, you have been adopted into the family of God. God sees you as His son. God loves you and is pleased with you. Hear that again. God loves you and is pleased with you. He is glad you are His child. Like He did with Jesus, He gladly and loudly proclaims, "That one is Mine! I love him! I'm proud of him."

Something about that truth touches us deeply. Our tendency is to quickly move past it and ignore what God is trying to do in us. And often, we feel unable to look at the Father and allow Him to say those words to us. But we must stop and allow the Father love of God to touch us deeply. We need to hear those words and believe them. You are His beloved son.

You Are a Friend

As you grow in your relationship with Christ, you remain both a slave and a son. It seems like those two cannot coexist, but they can. Paul, who referred to himself as a slave in Titus 1, is the same one who revealed our true sonship in Romans 8. You are a submissive slave and a beloved son. Both of these phrases communicate something different about the nature of your identity in Christ. And from there, we can begin to see ourselves as true friends.

In John 15, as Jesus taught His disciples about their need to continually abide in Him, He made an amazing statement.

Jesus said, "I do not call you servants anymore, because a servant doesn't know what his master is doing. I have called you friends, because I have made known to you everything I have heard from my Father" (v. 15 csb). Jesus calls you a friend. He wants a friendship with you.

This progression in our relationship with God is important. In a servant-master relationship, the master is clearly above the slave. The master tells the slave what to do, and the slave does it. There are no questions, no discussion, no debate. A servant does not know what his master is doing. That is not the nature of the relationship.

In a father-son relationship, the father is still above the son, but there is a relational closeness. There is love. There is affection. There is a family bond. There is the communication of affection and wisdom. There is instruction. There is still authority, but there is also relationship.

But Jesus goes beyond the father-son relationship and says He longs for friendship. The relationship of a friend moves from an authoritative, top-down relationship, to a side-by-side relationship. You are now walking together. In a friendship, you talk more openly, share more honestly, and just enjoy being together. You have a kind of closeness with a friend that you do not have with a father.

Jesus is inviting us into friendship. What an amazing thought. God is still the master of our lives. God is still a loving father who guides us in the way of wisdom. But He also invites us to walk with Him, enjoy His company, and enjoy an intimacy that only friends can experience. He enjoys your company and wants to spend time with you. He does not just want to be your Lord and your Father; He wants to be your friend.

Many men never get to this place in their relationship with God, and that's a shame. Many don't know how to be loving fathers because they have never known the Father love of God. In the same way, many are unable to have true friendships because they have never known friendship with God. When we learn to walk and talk with the Lord in openness and honesty, it allows us to do that with others.

We often resist those kinds of friendships. Our pride keeps us from that kind of honesty. But when we come to experience friendship with Jesus and let the walls of pride down in that relationship, it allows us to move into deeper earthly friendships. There is so much more that Jesus wants to experience with you. He is inviting you to enjoy that kind of relationship with Him. He really wants to be your friend (Matt. 11:19).

You Are a Lover

In 2013, while my wife was battling stage-4 cancer, something happened in me that I was not expecting: I began to fall in love with Jesus.

During that time, there was a popular worship song many churches were singing that was an intimate expression of love for Jesus. Our worship pastor wanted to sing it, but I kept telling him "no." It seemed feminine, overly emotional, and shallow to me. But throughout this journey through cancer, this song became the true expression of my heart. I listened to it over and over again. My cynicism toward these kinds of songs had been confronted with a new understanding of what it meant to love Jesus. Every man has been called to truly fall in love with Jesus. You were created to be a lover.

In a book on manhood, this is a hard concept to understand. I was explaining this to an older pastor friend and his response was simple, "That sounds way too feminine!" Yet, it is true, and it is essential. The church is the "bride of Christ" (Eph. 5:21–24). One day we will sit down at the marriage supper of the Lamb (Rev. 19:6–9). Paul said to the church in Corinth, "I am jealous for you with a godly jealousy. I promised you to one husband, to Christ, so that I might present you as a pure virgin to him" (2 Cor. 11:2 NIV). All of these statements are metaphors to help us understand the nature of our relationship with Jesus. He passionately loves us and is calling us to passionately love Him.

> Every man has been called to truly fall in love with Jesus.

When Jesus met with Peter, after Peter's denial and Jesus's resurrection, Jesus only asked Peter one question: Do you love

Me? When Jesus asked this question, He used two different words for love. The first two times Jesus asked Peter, He used the word *agape*, which is a more general word for unconditional love. But the third time, Jesus used the word *phileo*, which refers to a more relational, affectionate, and intimate love. What was Jesus doing? He was calling Peter into deeper love. This is what Jesus was doing in me during my wife's cancer, and it is what He wants to do in you.

Jesus is calling every man into a deeper, more intimate, more passionate love relationship. Jesus wants you to fall in love with Him. After all, the first and greatest commandment is to have a passionate, all-consuming love for God (Matt. 22:37). The continual call of God on every man of God is to love Him more and more. And the reality is, if a man does not understand how to love God, he will never learn how to love his wife, his children, or his neighbor. You have been created to be a passionate lover, and the truest men are those who love the most deeply and passionately. Starting with your love for God.

I was talking to a friend of mine recently who was deeply wounded by his father, who was a local church pastor. My friend is in his early fifties and still carries those wounds. But they are not the wounds of things done as much as the wounds of things not done. They were the wounds of never really knowing his father. Although they grew up in the same home, they never really knew each other. My friend never felt the acceptance, affection, and affirmation he needed from his father.

Why was this father, like so many fathers, unable to give these things to his son? I believe the root issue is most men never move beyond master-servant relationship with Jesus. They have learned to be a slave and are submissive to the Lord, but they do not know God as a Father, much less God as friend or lover. And the reason some of this language seems foreign and strange to many men is because if you have never known God as anything more than a master, it is hard to see others, including your children, as anything but slaves.

Seeing yourself as a servant is the starting place of a relationship with Jesus. The first call of Jesus is to follow Him. We respond by submitting ourselves to Him as a slave. But this is just the starting place. As we come to know Jesus more, He calls us into a deeper relationship. He is calling you into sonship, friendship, and intimate love. He is calling you to move toward intimacy. And as we move in that direction toward God, we will be able to move in that direction toward others.

Becoming What You Are

These four aspects of our identity—servant, son, friend, and lover—are just the tip of the iceberg. You are so much more. You are a saint, a new creation, an ambassador, a gifted part of the body, a family member, and a sojourner. And the most amazing part is, you are all of those at the same time! That truth is not meant to overwhelm you, it is meant to empower you. You are so much more than you ever imagined. And God is calling you into the daily experience of each of your identities in Christ.

There may be seasons of life in which God is continually calling you into deeper sonship. Times in which you need more affirmation and wisdom. There may be times in which He is calling you into a deeper friendship. Times in which you need more closeness. There are times when God will call you, as a member of a local church, into more of your role in God's family. God is always calling you into more of your true identity.

The key is this: *you must keep discovering who you are through His Word.* Allow God to define you. Don't let anyone else or anything else define you. You are not defined by your past. You are not defined by what others said about you. You are not defined by your limitations. You are defined by God. And the more time you spend in His Word, the more you will come to realize just who you truly are.

You must listen for those phrases that have been stuck in your mind for years and stop allowing them to define you. You must take those thoughts captive (2 Cor. 10:5). You must replace the curse of words with the blessing of your true identity in Jesus Christ. To do that, you must allow yourself the time and space to let God speak deeply into your heart, through His Word and by the power of His Spirit, and redefine you.

Beware of the Vicious Cycle

Let me end with one warning. If you do not understand and live out of your identity in Christ, there will be a serious cost. A man who does not understand his own identity cannot be the husband, father, leader, or church member God wants him to be. You cannot be the father God wants you to be unless you know the Father love of God. You cannot be the friend you need to be unless you have experienced friendship with God. You cannot love your wife unless you have learned how to love and be loved by God.

> A man who does not understand his own identity cannot be the husband, father, leader, or church member God wants him to be.

But beyond that, there is a subtler cycle a man gets into when he does not know who he is in Christ. Those who do not know their true identity get into a cycle of comparing, coveting, and competing.

You will continually compare yourself, your family, your job, your finances, your gifts with other men around you. Honestly, you will end up obsessed with comparison.

Comparison always leads to coveting. This is a subtle but certain shift. As you compare your life to someone else's, you will begin to covet what they have. Our comparing makes us think that what others have is better than what we have. Most likely, it's not. Every person we compare ourselves to has just as many issues and problems as we do.

Comparing and coveting always lead to competing. You know this is true. Men love to compete—not just on the field, but in life. Many men are driven by their desire to have more than other men. To have a better job, a better car, a nicer home, or a more successful child. When you think about it, it's just a pitiful cycle. But it's the certain cycle of every man who does not have his identity settled and established in Jesus Christ.

Let Jesus redefine you. Every moment of every day. Remind yourself of who you are. Immerse yourself in His Word so that He is the one who is whispering in your ear your true identity. Then, remind yourself. Tell yourself all the time. And continue to grow in that reality until the Lord takes you home. And as you do, feel yourself becoming a more whole and solid man.

Discussion Questions

1. What part of this chapter stirred your heart the most? Yes, be specific.

2. Have you ever experienced the curse of words? How has that affected you? Specifics!

3. How do you most often view God: Master, Father, Friend, or Lover? Which one is most difficult for you? Why?

4. How far have you moved in your relationship with Jesus? Meaning, have you only experienced Him as a master or have you experienced Him as a friend?

Chapter 4

ASSIGNMENTS

ONE OF THE healthiest habits a man can cultivate is the daily reading of the book of Proverbs. This book is more than just practical wisdom for daily living and decision making. Proverbs shows us how to walk in the way of wisdom, becoming a wise person. And since Jesus is the wisdom of God (1 Cor. 1:24), the book of Proverbs is really a guide for how to trust and follow Jesus.

Although Proverbs contains godly wisdom for every believer, it contains some very specific wisdom for men. The book was written from a father to a son, instructing him on how to trust and follow the Lord on the pathway of wisdom (Prov. 1:8). And in some very specific ways it shows men how to avoid much of the folly of youth (see Proverbs 5 and 7).

One of the distinct features of the book that makes it so compelling is the different characters. There are the wise, the fool, the simple, the scoffer, the glutton, the diligent, and more. One of the saddest characters, and the most colorful, is the sluggard. The sluggard puts his hand in his dish, but is too lazy to bring it back to his mouth (Prov. 26:15). He is so lazy that he refuses to get up and go to work, and justifies his laziness by making up a story about a lion being outside (22:13). The sluggard is a pitiful character.

A few years ago, I noticed that among all the colorful characters in Proverbs, there is no reference to a workaholic. No mention at all. And in a book primarily written as a manual for life from a father to a son, it seems strange that there was no warning to the son of becoming a workaholic. Certainly some men, like the sluggard, work too little. But other men work too much. Many men have destroyed their own life, and the lives of those around them, by sacrificing their family on the altar of success. How could this not even get one verse?

Eventually, I realized the reason there is no mention of a workaholic in the book of Proverbs is because there isn't such a thing. We use the term *workaholic* to refer to a man who works so much that he sacrifices other important things in his life. But the issue is not that he is addicted to work. There is a deeper issue.

> A man who is a workaholic is really just a sluggard at home.

A man who is a workaholic is really just a sluggard at home. A man who is viewed as a hard worker might, in reality, be lazy.

He's working hard at his job to avoid the harder work that needs to be done at home.

A man who neglects his church, his family, and even his own health for work has failed to put the same kind of effort into things that matter more. His life is not in order. He does not have boundaries. He is not driven by a sense of priority. Parts of his life might be thriving while other important areas are falling apart. Many men live this way, but they don't have to. Every man can live a purposeful and priority-driven life where that which matters most is getting the most attention. But in order to do so, a man must understand his God-given assignments.

Identity vs. Assignments

Many of a man's struggles are directly related to their lack of a clear identity. If you do not have a clear identity, you will allow your past, your failures, your success, the words of others, or the expectations of others to define you. You will live your life comparing yourself to others and competing with others. Your life will feel like a treadmill of uncertainty that never stops. It's exhausting.

You must settle the issue of identity, and you do that by allowing the gospel to redefine you. Your identity is who you are in Christ. It is the foundation for everything else in your life. Your effectiveness, confidence, ambitions, and focus all flow out of your identity. If you do not know who you are, you will never become the man God wants you to be. You must be able to answer, with confidence, the question, "Who am I?"

Once your identity becomes clear, you must get clarity on your assignments. Identity answers the question, "Who am I?" Assignments answer the question, "What has God called me to do?" Identity never changes. Assignments often change. Identity must be held tightly. Assignments must be held loosely. Identity is about being. Assignments are about doing.

Identity and assignments are distinct but inseparable. Your identity is the foundation for understanding and accomplishing your assignments. You will never fully understand, embrace, or properly function in your God-given assignments without proper identity. And, if you do not understand your identity first, then your assignments will become your identity. Then, when your assignments become your identity, you'll have an identity crisis when God changes your assignment. Many struggles come in a man's life when he does not know the difference between his identity and his assignments.

As Paul begins his letter to Titus, he gives both his identity and his assignment. He says, "Paul, a servant of God and an apostle of Jesus Christ" (Titus 1:1). In those simple words, he shows he understands the difference between his identity and his assignments. His identity is a

> Identity is about being. Assignments are about doing.

servant of God. His assignment is an apostle of God. A servant is who he is. An apostle is what he does.

Much of Paul's confidence and effectiveness in his life and ministry is a result of his clear understanding of the distinct and inseparable nature of these two things. Our confidence and effectiveness will come from the same clarity.

God-Given Assignments

Your assignments are anything God has entrusted to you and called you to do. Thinking in terms of dominion, assignments are the specific domains which God has called you to work and keep. Every one of your God-given assignments will fall under one of the primary domains: your self, your church, your family, and your work. But, in order to live out a sense of purpose, you must be more specific than that.

Identifying specific jobs and people as "God-given assignments" is a game-changer. Seeing your family as a God-given assignment gives a great sense of purpose and responsibility. It also takes many of the mundane, everyday parts of your life and turns them into very specific callings God has given you. As a result, you will live out of a sense of calling and will give your assignments the time, attention, and thought they deserve.

When you see your life through the lens of your God-given assignments, you might also realize you are spending a significant amount of time on things that are not God-given assignments. You might even find you are sacrificing many of your God-given assignments for things that are of less value and are not a primary part of your calling. In discovering that, you might rearrange your priorities, giving those lesser things less attention and giving the greater things more attention.

My father-in-law loves to play golf. Well, at least that's what I had always thought. When I got into the family, golf was a big part of every family vacation, and as a result, most family conversations. I even went to Scotland with my father-in-law and three brothers-in-law to play at St. Andrews and Carnoustie—two of the oldest and most famous courses in the world.

One day I asked him when he got into golf. He explained to me that he's not passionate about golf; he is passionate about his three sons, and his three sons enjoy golf. So, in a desire to build deep and lasting relationships with his sons, he started playing golf. If you ask him to play golf and his sons are not involved, he will most likely turn you down. He doesn't care that much about golf. But he is serious about his sons.

My father-in-law saw his three sons as one of his primary and most important God-given assignments. Golf was just a means to an end. Golf was just a way to fulfill a greater assignment. Because he saw this distinction so clearly, he was able to enjoy golf, use it as a means to invest in his sons, and never allow it to take away from his time with his sons. That is why understanding your assignments matters so much.

You need clarity on your assignments. True manhood demands it. You must continue to resist the urge to just exist, to thoughtlessly move from one thing to the next, and to just passively let life happen. You must see what matters most in life and give yourself fully to those things while ruthlessly eliminating what does not matter.

Life is too short to be vague about your assignments. Every man must know his assignments, be able to prioritize those assign-ments, and believe God has given him what he needs to fulfill those assignments.

> Life is too short to be vague about your assignments.

Knowing Your Assignments

This idea of God-given assignments might be new to you. Clarifying these assignments might take some time, thought, and prayer, but it is an important step. I want to ask you to take the time to write these assignments down. Writing this down is extremely important. This is where you start to get a sense of God's calling on your life.

Remember, a God-given assignment is anyone God has entrusted to you and anything He called you to do. For instance, your wife is *your* God-given assignment, not any-one else's. Your children are *your* God-given assignment, not anyone else's. Your ministry within your local church, your job, school, and your grandchildren are part of *your* assignments.

Your assignments are the responsibilities or people that have been entrusted to your care. To think about it in terms of your true manhood, what areas of your life have you been called to use your plow and your sword? Don't think in vague terms; be specific.

At this point, don't worry about priority. Right now, just write down everyone God has entrusted to you and everything God has called you to do. Think about it this way: What are the things in life that, if you neglected them, would indicate you had not been faithful to the Lord? You might be surprised what is on this list. You might also be surprised what is not on this list.

Walking Carefully

The book of Proverbs is replete with admonitions to think carefully about our life and the use of our time. Proverbs 4:25–26 says, "Let your eyes look directly forward, and your gaze be straight before you. Ponder the path of your feet; then all your ways will be sure." The word *ponder* means "to give careful thought and consideration." Proverbs 16:9 says, "The heart of man plans his way, but the LORD establishes his steps." The second part of that verse tells us to hold our plans loosely because, as we all know, God might very well change them. But the first part of that verse teaches us that, although God might change our plans, a wise man makes plans.

Maybe the apostle Paul says it clearer when he says, "Look carefully then how you walk, not as unwise but as wise, making the best use of the time, because the days are evil. Therefore, do not be foolish, but understand what the will of the Lord is" (Eph. 5:15–17).

Clearly, God expects us to think carefully about our life, our plans, and our time. A thoughtless life is a foolish life.

This means that the Christian walk demands something we don't often want to give—careful thought. We don't like to stop and ponder. We are too busy. But walking with Jesus demands it. We will never live a purposeful, productive, and priority-driven life without careful thought. And there is no area in which this is more true than the area of our God-given assignments.

When I first started talking to men about assignments, I would not only ask them to write down their assignments, I would have them list those assignments in order of priority. I like the simplicity of that. Life would demand so much less thought if we could just make a clean and clear list of every assignment in order of priority. But unfortunately, life is just not that simple.

Life is complicated. That's why we have to think carefully about how we walk. It's why we have to "ponder."

Prioritizing our assignments is complicated. We must think carefully about it. Not only because priorities matter, but because the priority of our assignments changes.

I have five children who still live at home. At this season in my life, my children are one of my top priorities. People often ask me if I have any hobbies. I tell them that my children are my hobby. It's true. Maybe someday I will have time to pick up some other hobbies, but not right now. Of course, for single men and empty nesters, the priorities are different. Priorities change in different seasons of life.

Priorities also change from week to week. There are weeks when you will need to say "no" to something with the family in order to say "yes" to something at church. There will also be weeks when you need to say "no" to something at church in order to say "yes" to something with the family. There are times when you need to leave a meeting early in order to make it to a child's game. There are also times in which you have to skip a game for an important meeting.

These are not easy decisions. And yet, they are decisions that must be made. If we don't take this kind of thoughtful approach to life, we will inevitably waste our life. A thoughtful approach to life is complicated, but that complication is actually a blessing. Those complications force us into a more intentional life.

How do you know what needs priority from week to week? You think carefully how you walk. The first time I ever thought about this was when I heard a pastor talk about a Sunday evening discipline he had cultivated over the years. Before starting the week, he would look at his calendar and his assignments and plan out his week accordingly. At first, this seemed like overkill, and during certain seasons, it might be. But for most of us, this is exactly the kind of careful thought that our life demands. If we do not cultivate a habit like this, our lives will continually feel out of balance and important things will always get neglected.

Questions to Ask

In order to live a priority-driven life, in which you are faithfully fulfilling your God-given assignments, you must continually ask a series of important questions. Questions like:

- Are any of my God-given assignments suffering right now because they are not getting enough of my attention?

- What things do I need to say "no" to this week, and what things do I need to say "yes" to?
- Are there any assignments that need more specific attention right now?
- Are there any assignments I am avoiding right now for any reason?
- Are any of my assignments suffering because of the amount of time I am spending on something that is not an assignment?
- What should my priorities be this week?

When you ask questions like this, you are ensuring that you are not mindlessly living every day while important things are suffering. Questions like this allow you to live a well-ordered and productive life in which those things that matter most get the most attention. If you fail to ask questions like this, you will one day feel the rippling effects of a thoughtless life.

In a sense, what you are doing when you ask questions like this is budgeting your time. Like money, you have a limited amount of time every week. And like money, without a plan, that time will go quickly and you will accomplish less than you would like. So, like with money, if you want that time to be spent wisely and to have enough to accomplish what you need to, you make a budget. Instead of being a burden, that budget actually leads you to great freedom and a sense of purpose.

Since the priority of our assignments not only changes by season, but by week, these are questions that need to be asked continually. Ideally, we would ask these questions each week as we plan for the week ahead.

Asking questions like these on a regular basis also ensures that you are continually submitting your will, your time, and your life to the direction of the Lord. This forces us to listen to the Lord and make wise decisions. It is learning how to live moment by moment under the direction of the Spirit of God.

Don't Forget the Church

As you are thinking about your assignments, I want to challenge you to think carefully about something we discussed briefly in chapter one. It is the place and priority of the local church in your life.

The book of Titus addresses three main issues: the church, the home, and the workplace. The first thing Paul tells Titus to get in order is the church—not the home. Even though there were problems in the home (Titus 1:11; 2:1–6), the first priority was the church. Healthy families grow out of healthy churches. The first place he calls a man to work and keep is the church—not the home.

We grieve over the breakdown of the nuclear family in America. And we should. This breakdown is having unimaginable effects on the coming generations, and our nation as a whole. The breakdown of the family certainly leads to the breakdown of society. But I rarely hear anyone grieving the breakdown of the local church, and the breakdown of the local church has a far greater impact on the world, and on eternity, than does any nuclear family.

One of the most important passages in regards to the relationship between the nuclear family and the church family is Ephesians 5:22–33. There are many things to be said about this relationship, but the clearest truth is that the nuclear family exists for the glory of Christ and His church. In other words, God created nuclear families to reveal the greater reality of the church family, not the other way around. The health of our marriage and family matters so much because they exist to point to the greater relationship between Christ and the church.

The church is eternal, but the nuclear family is temporal. Heaven will be a place in which the universal church is all finally gathered and will be gathered for eternity, but there will be no marriage in heaven (Matt. 22:30). This is because God created the nuclear family as a little picture of that which is of most value and of that which is eternal.

I am not sure how we lost our way on this issue, but we have. We are raising a generation of children in the church who, because of how little their parents prioritize the church, are growing up believing that the church is of little significance. This will have greater harm on their future, the future of their families, and the future of our society, than any other positive things we might try to re-enforce.

In practical terms, this looks like making sure you are an identifiable and active member of a local church. Meaning, you know you are a member of the church and the church knows you are a member. You attend regularly, giving sacrificially, participating in the church's mission, and have an identifiable area of ministry in which you are serving. It means that your family knows that the local church matters and is a priority. And not out of a sense of drudgery or duty, but out of an awareness that the local church is the body and bride of Christ Himself.

One of the most defining moments in my childhood was a moment when I smarted off to my mom in front of my dad. At that moment, my dad made it very clear, in no uncertain terms, that although that woman was my mom, she was also his wife. He would not stand idly and watch as someone disrespected his wife—including his own thirteen-year-old son. That was a big moment for me. As strange as it seems, I had never thought about my mom as my dad's wife. My dad was right. And his passion for his wife was a lesson I needed to learn.

Men, the church is not only the very body of Christ, the church is the bride of Christ. Do you think Jesus cares about the way we treat His bride? Do you think His bride matters to Him? Do you think He passively looks the other way when we disregard His bride? Men, not only is the health of your family tied to your commitment to the local church, your walk with Jesus is tied to your commitment to the local church. Let's give her the attention she deserves.

God Has What It Takes

When we begin to get clarity on our assignments, and begin to think carefully about how to prioritize them, we might begin to feel both overwhelmed and inadequate. That's understandable. And I would say, those are good and healthy first responses to understanding and fulfilling your God-given assignments.

The overwhelmed feeling comes from the sense that there are more things to do than there is time to do them. For years I lived with the constant feeling I had more to do than I had time to do it. When people asked me how I was doing, I would immediately tell them how busy I was. I just lived with the feeling that I was never doing enough and could never get everything done. But at some point, the Lord taught me a little truth: God has given me enough time to do everything He has called me to do.

I may not have time to do everything I need to do and a bunch of other things I'd like to do, but I do have enough time to do everything God has called me to do. This has to be true. If it wasn't true, then it would be an indictment on the sufficiency of God. God has given you sufficient time to do everything He has called you to do.

One of the greatest gifts my father gave me was the gift of a work ethic. Throughout my adult life I have looked back at how my father made me work and have found myself overwhelmingly grateful. I hated it growing up, but I am so thankful now.

Working hard is a real value for me. I am convinced that few things destroy a man's life more than passivity and laziness. God created us to work. And work hard. But over the years I have come to discover the real virtue is not hard work. There are a lot of men who work hard but neglect things that matter most. The real virtue is a disciplined work ethic.

In order to fulfill your God-given assignments, you must have a disciplined work ethic. But it must be a disciplined work ethic. You must be disciplined to wake up early and spend time with Jesus. Then go to work and give yourself fully to whatever work God has assigned to you. Then come home and give your best to your wife and children. Then, after the day's work is done, sleep well.

Jim Elliot, who was martyred at age twenty-eight while trying to reach the Huaorani tribe in Ecuador, famously wrote in his journal, "Wherever you are, be all there! Live to the hilt every situation you believe to be the will of God." In order to fulfill your God given assignments, you must learn to "be all there."

Because of our phones, when we are at work, our minds are often at home. When we are at home, our minds are often at work. And often, when we are at home or work, our minds are miles away focusing on someone else's life on social media. We are often physically in a room filled with people who matter to us, while our minds are focused on people we don't even care that much about.

In order to fulfill your calling, you need to be fully present, in every moment, doing exactly what needs to be done in that moment. Instead of feeling overwhelmed by what needs to be done, simply do what needs to be done that's right in front of us. God has given us enough time, but we must be present in it. Be all there!

When you look at your assignments, you might also feel inadequate. I'm not sure I've ever talked to a man who didn't feel inadequate in some area of his life.

A man who is highly successful at his work might feel like a total failure at home. He might avoid being home because he feels so inadequate. He stays at work because that is where he feels confident. But inadequacy is not our enemy. Inadequacy is a gift. Inadequacy is that feeling that exists to draw you to greater dependence, not lead you to greater passivity (2 Cor. 2:16).

In one of the most liberating and helpful texts of Scripture, the apostle Paul makes it clear that the secret to his strength was his utter sense of inadequacy (2 Cor. 12:1–10).

The reason you feel so inadequate is that you are. Without question, you don't have what it takes to fulfill all these assignments. But God does. And God wants to use your weakness to drive you to Himself, and then, in Him, to find the strength and wisdom you need.

Instead of allowing your sense of inadequacy to keep you from your God-given assignments, allow it to draw you to the Lord, where you will find all the sufficiency you need. Instead of ignoring the thought it takes to discern your priorities, spend time prayerfully pondering them.

Here is the point: God has everything you need (time, attention, energy, resources) to do everything He has called you to do. You don't, but He does. He is the vine; you are the branch. He desires that you stay so united with Him, so closely connected to Him, that the fulfillment of your God-given assignments is a picture of the very life of Jesus flowing through you. This is the way He always intended it to be.

So, next time you feel completely inadequate, don't run away from the place of inadequacy. Stop, and thank the Lord for that feeling. Then ask for His grace, wisdom, and strength to complete the assignments He has given you, for His glory.

Fulfill Your Assignment

In 1 Corinthians 3, the apostle Paul confronted a ridiculous debate going on in the church of Corinth. Some people in the church were saying, "I follow Paul," while others were saying, "I follow Apollos." Paul's response to the church is really helpful for us.

Paul says, "What then is Apollos? What is Paul? Servants through whom you believed, as the Lord assigned to each" (v. 5). Did you catch that last phrase? "As the Lord assigned to each." Each person has been given an assignment by God. God fulfills His work through a multitude of people who are just faithful with their assignment.

You have one job every day—fulfill your God-given assignments to the best of your ability to the glory of God. May the Lord give us the clarity and discipline to do that.

Discussion Questions

1. In your current season of life, what are some of your most important God-given assignments?

2. Which of those assignments are the most challenging for you? Why?

3. Honestly, where does church rank in the order of your priorities? How could you make it a greater priority?

4. Which of your assignments make you feel the most overwhelmed or inadequate? Why?

Chapter 5

AUTHORITY

IN HIS 1867 inaugural address at the University of St. Andrews, John Stuart Mill said, "Let not anyone pacify his conscience by the delusion that he can do no harm if he takes no part, and forms no opinion. Bad men need nothing more to compass their ends, than that good men would look on and do nothing." This phrase seems to be the source of the quote by Edmund Burke: "The only thing necessary for the triumph of evil is for good men to do nothing."

It is not only the things a man does that can have a damaging effect on others; more often, it is what a man fails to do that causes the greatest harm. Could it be that the greatest damage a man can do to himself, his family, his church, and his community, is to do nothing?

There is an epidemic among men. It is destroying men, families, churches, and communities at an alarming rate. It is the epidemic of *passivity*.

It isn't new. It has been around since the creation of man. It's what infected Adam when he stood by and allowed the Serpent to deceive Eve. Sin came into the world while Adam watched and did nothing. And it seems from that moment on, the enemy knew he could wreak havoc on the world if he could just get men to be passive.

I saw a video on the news recently of a woman being assaulted by a man in public. It was incredibly disturbing. As a man with four daughters, there is nothing that stirs up more righteous anger in me than the abuse of women.

I normally turn these videos off, but in just a moment, something in the video caught my attention. I couldn't help but notice the number of men who stood by and watched the assault take place, many of them recording it on their phones instead of intervening.

In a much subtler way, that scene is played out millions of times in millions of homes, churches, and communities every day. Every day, men stand by as those around them are assaulted, without doing anything. And as much as we despise the men in that video who stood by and watched, at times, all of us tend to do the same.

> Every day, men stand by as those around them are assaulted, without doing anything.

A Subtle Assault

The greatest assault on our lives and the lives of those around us is the subtle and silent spiritual assault of Satan. It might seem like a less troubling assault than the woman on the street, but it's just as disturbing and damaging. Many men, who would never stand back and watch their wife or child be physically assaulted, will stand by while they are being spiritually assaulted.

Because this is a spiritual assault, it is much more difficult to see the damage caused by our inaction. Our passivity seems harmless. The reason is, much like Adam in the garden, we don't see what's at stake when we are passive. I don't think Adam ever imagined the long-term consequences of his inactivity. But he should have. His passivity was only matched by his obliviousness. He had no excuse.

We will never see how damaging our passivity is unless we understand how real the assault, and the assaulter is. Ephesians 6 says,

> Finally, be strong in the Lord and in the strength of his might. Put on the whole armor of God, that you may be able to stand against the schemes of the devil. For we do not wrestle against flesh and blood, but against the rulers, against the authorities, against the cosmic powers over this present darkness, against the

spiritual forces of evil in the heavenly places. Therefore, take up the whole armor of God, that you may be able to withstand in the evil day, and having done all, to stand firm. (Eph. 6:10–13)

We tend to think our greatest struggles are with the people and situations we can see. But according to Ephesians 6, our greatest battle is an unseen one that is being waged in the spiritual places. Jesus said, "The thief comes only to steal and kill and destroy" (John 10:10). This was not hyperbole. Jesus is talking about a very real enemy who has plans to destroy you, your family, your church, and your community. And he is not passive!

Satan is aggressive, subtle, and smart. You must actively resist him. Peter says, "Be sober-minded; be watchful. Your adversary the devil prowls around like a roaring lion, seeking someone to devour. Resist him, firm in your faith, knowing that the same kinds of suffering are being experienced by your brotherhood throughout the world" (1 Pet. 5:8–9).

Do you believe that? Honestly. *Do you believe that?*

Do you believe there is a very real enemy out there who is daily assaulting you, and his goal is to devour you? Do you see how

> Satan is aggressive, subtle, and smart. You must actively resist him.

this type of spiritual assault could be more eternally damaging than any physical assault?

Peter's use of imagery is interesting. Why would he choose a lion as a picture of how Satan wants to devour us? Because lions are brilliant and fierce hunters. The imagery reveals how dangerous the enemy is. He knows how to hunt and devour. The reality of this demonic lion should make us vigilant.

Satan wins when we are passive. Peter is clear that we can defend ourselves against him if we choose to. He does not have to win; his power is real, but limited nonetheless. He wins when we fail to be sober-minded, watchful, and active in resisting him.

Passively Allowing Assault

What if your tendency toward spiritual passivity was allowing you and those around you to be assaulted in unimaginable ways with unimaginable consequences? What if all the little things you are not doing are more damaging than the things you are doing? What if, like Adam, you are standing aside while those you love are easy prey for the lion? This happens every day. It happens in moments like this:

- You are struggling with pornography. You resist community and Christian friendship. Instead, you begin to isolate yourself. You fail to confess your sins, and refuse accountability. You hide from God, and others.

- You have a problem with anger. You know it. Your family knows it. You know you need help. But you keep it a secret, and the anger continues to grow.
- You have an argument with your wife. It does not end well. Anger and resentment begin to well up inside of you. You know you need to talk it out, but you choose to do the easy thing—nothing.
- You know there are ethical issues in your company, but ignoring them will lead to fewer problems. So, you look the other way.
- You hear one of your children talk back to your wife. Your wife tries to get him to obey, but he ignores her. You just got home from work, you're tired, and you don't want to deal with it. So, you don't.
- Your daughter pushes back when you tell her that what she is wearing is immodest. You know she shouldn't wear it, but you can't stand seeing her disappointed, so you give in.

- Your teenage children don't feel like going to church. So, you let them make their own decisions.
- There is gossip in the church that you know is wrong. You hear it—you're even on the receiving end of it—but you don't confront it. You decide to act like you don't know anything about it, or shrug it off like it's no big deal.

These types of situations might seem harmless, but this is exactly how the enemy works. This is how the enemy begins to assault you or the ones you love. Just think about the case of the unresolved argument with your wife. Leaving that unresolved is certainly easier. None of us wants to get into a long conversation at 10 p.m. But not dealing with it gives the enemy a foothold in your marriage and will lead to greater issues. Your passivity has allowed the enemy to assault you, your wife, and your family.

> Godly men don't do what is easy; they do what is right.

Passivity is always easier. But godly men don't do what is easy; they do what is right.

What is the solution to this passivity? How can we take our stand and protect ourselves and those we love? How can we remain firm against those kinds of demonic assaults?

Instead of walking in fleshly passivity, God is calling you to walk in kingdom authority.

Kingdom Authority

My favorite verse in Titus is the last verse of chapter 2. Titus had been given an incredibly difficult and complicated assignment. He was to identify new leaders and openly oppose the ungodly men in the church and silence them. Then, in chapter 2 Paul tells Titus to give specific instruction to the older men, older women, younger men, and younger women. He is then to help them understand the nature of the gospel and how it is to transform them into people who are zealous for God.

Now, after telling Titus all the things he needed to do, the people he needed to confront, and the changes he needed to make, Paul says this: "Declare these things; exhort and rebuke with all authority. Let no one disregard you" (Titus 2:15). Paul knew that Titus was walking into a battle. This entire church had been assaulted by godless and rebellious men who were destroying it from the inside out. They had to be dealt with. Passivity was not an option. Titus had to walk in his God-given kingdom authority.

Your Kingdom Authority

In Luke 9, Jesus sends out His inexperienced disciples to proclaim the gospel and heal. They had been watching Him do these things, and now it was their turn. As He sent them out, He gave them two indispensable things: power and authority.

Today, Christ has given you the same two weapons to use as you seek to be a man of God and advance the kingdom of God. In Matthew 28:18–20, Jesus leaves you with authority. In Acts 1:8, He gives you power. With His power and authority, God has given you *everything* you need to be the man He has called you to be and fulfill the work He has called you to do. Without these two, you don't have a chance.

If you grew up in church, you most likely learned about power—the kind of power that flows from the filling of God's Spirit and is given for the fulfillment of God's mission. Without the filling of the Holy Spirit, you will never manifest the life of Jesus Christ or accomplish the work of Christ. Although the Holy Spirit gets less attention than the Father and the Son, most of us are at least familiar with the power of the Spirit.

But sadly, most people have never thought about authority. Yet, the authority of Jesus and the authority given to every believer in Jesus is just as crucial for you in fulfilling your God-given assignments as the power of the Spirit.

Kingdom authority can be defined this way: *Kingdom authority is the right and responsibility to act and rule under the king, on behalf of the king, and for the king.*

A man of God does not have the right to be passive. This is why understanding authority at this point in the book is so crucial. We began with the understanding that God has called you to take dominion. In reality, kingdom authority is just the godly expression of dominion. But you cannot walk in *authority*—the expression of *dominion*—unless you understand both your *identity* and your *assignments.*

Understanding your identity first makes you realize you only have authority because it has been given to you as a person who has been brought into the kingdom through the death, burial, and resurrection of Jesus. You only have kingdom authority because it has been given to you by the King. And the only way you know where and how to express that authority is if you understand your assignments. Now that you do understand you have been called (1) to take dominion, (2) to participate as a citizen of the kingdom, and (3) to take on your God-given assignments, you must know how to walk in your God-given kingdom authority.

> Kingdom authority is the right and responsibility to act and rule under the king, on behalf of the king, and for the king.

The Kingdom Authority of Jesus

There is no greater example of kingdom authority than the earthly life and ministry of Jesus. Jesus reveals to us what it means to walk both under authority and in authority. We see this most clearly in the story of the centurion who came to Jesus and asked that his servant be healed. He said,

> "Lord, my servant is lying paralyzed at home, suffering terribly." And he said to him, "I will come and heal him." But the centurion replied, "Lord, I am not worthy to have you come under my roof, but only say the word, and my servant will be healed. For I too am a man under authority, with soldiers under me. And I say to one, 'Go,' and he goes, and to another, 'Come,' and he comes, and to my servant, 'Do this,' and he does it." (Matt. 8:6–9)

This centurion would have understood authority. As the leader of around 100 men, he understood what it means to be in authority. When he told his men to do something, they did it. But, as a part of a much larger legion, he also understood what it meant to be under authority. When his leader told him what to do, he did it. He was in authority and under authority. When he approached Jesus, he viewed Jesus in the same way. And Jesus marveled at his discernment.

Jesus consistently talked about being a man under authority. John records more of these statements than anyone. Jesus regularly talked about His inability to do anything without the Father and His commitment to accomplish nothing but the will of the Father (John 5:30–36; 6:35–39; 12:44–50). Jesus even said that He did not speak on His authority, but on the authority of the one who sent Him (John 14:1–14). Jesus lived as a man under authority.

And yet, no one expressed more authority than Jesus. In Mark 1 alone, Jesus demonstrated His authority over temptation (vv. 12–13), in His teaching (v. 22), over demons (vv. 21–26), and over sickness (vv. 29–34). Jesus was a man called to walk under authority and in authority. And so are we.

Walking Under Authority

The reason we are often hesitant to talk about walking in authority is that we have seen so many abuses of authority. We also might have seen many misunderstandings of kingdom authority within the church. Many of you might have grown up in homes in which the expression of your father's authority was anything but loving and life-giving. Many people grow up in churches, communities, and countries where leaders abused their authority to the detriment of all those under them. But the reason authority is most often abused is that men try to walk *in* authority without walking *under* authority.

To walk under authority means to walk in complete submission to the Lord Jesus Christ.

When we choose to trust and follow Jesus, we are saying, "I surrender myself fully to You." And this is not a one-time declaration. This is our daily disposition. Our very identity as a follower of Jesus is that we no longer belong to ourselves, but to the one who called us to Himself (1 Cor. 6:20).

But not only do you live as fully surrendered servants of the Lord Jesus Christ, you also live in daily dependence upon the Lord Jesus Christ. Surrender says, "I do nothing on my own." Dependence says, "I can do nothing on my own." You live like a branch that receives all of your life from the vine (John 15:1–8). Your only hope of manifesting the life of Jesus is found in walking in continual communion with Him.

Living as one under authority means you are ready, willing, and even eager to be radically obedient to Jesus. Jesus said to His Father, "I glorified you on earth, having accomplished the work that you gave me to do" (John 17:4). We are called to be good soldiers, ready to engage in any battle God calls us into. Like Titus, we must be willing to step into the battle and walk in our authority when God tells us to.

Men of God are not looking for conflict. We are not eager for it. But we are eager to do whatever God calls us to do. And when God calls us to step into a battle and walk in our God-given authority, it is only because we are doing so by His calling and for His glory.

You don't have a right to be passive. You are not your own; you have been bought with a price (1 Cor. 6:19–20). Passivity is refusing to live as if you are under the control of Jesus Christ. It is acting as if you are your own man with no regard to the fact that you exist for Jesus. Passivity is not just a bad habit; it is rebellion against God.

Here is the key: you cannot be over the things God wants you to be over unless you are under the things God wants you to be under. You cannot lead yourself, your family, your church, or any other area of life unless you are being led by the Spirit of God. You must get yourself in a proper position of humble submission, receiving your orders from King Jesus, and then walking in obedience to whatever He calls you to do. And if you live under the authority of Jesus and under the control of the Spirit, your expression of authority will always manifest the life of God.

> You cannot be over the things God wants you to be over unless you are under the things God wants you to be under.

Walking in Authority

The more you walk under authority, the more you are able to walk in authority. This is true because as you walk in authority you will be sensitive to the call of Jesus. You will no longer be passive, but aggressive in your obedience to Jesus. But what does this look like?

First, you express your authority by standing. You must aggressively take your stand against the enemy.

Think about your identity in Christ. You have been united with Jesus Christ in His death, burial, and resurrection. Because of this, you can consider yourself dead to sin and alive in Christ Jesus (Rom. 6). But did you realize that you are also united with Jesus in His ascension? Listen to these words,

> But God, being rich in mercy, because of the great love with which he loved us, even when we were dead in our trespasses, made us alive together with Christ—by grace, you have been saved—and raised us up with him and seated us with him in the heavenly places in Christ Jesus. (Eph. 2:4–6)

Paul already told them that Christ is seated "far above all rule and authority and power and dominion, and above every name that is named, not only in this age but also in the one to come" (Eph. 1:21).

What that means is that in the same way you are united with Jesus in His death and resurrection, making you dead to sin and alive in Him, you are united in His ascension, giving you authority over all of your enemies in the heavenly places.

The first and primary place in which we express our authority is over sin and Satan. This is how we take our stand against the devil's schemes (Eph. 6:10–11), stand firm against him (1 Pet. 5:8–9), and resist him (James 4:7). What in the world gives you the power to fight against sin and the attacks of the enemy? The authority you have as one who is united with Christ.

I am so tired of watching Satan destroy marriages, children, and churches while men stand by like there's nothing they can do. If you believe what Jesus says about the devil, then you know the enemy wants to destroy everything and everyone in your life. If you believe what Jesus says about your union with Him, you know you have the right and responsibility to take your stand against Satan.

When is the last time you think Satan tried to hurt you, your family, or your church? When is the last time you engaged in spiritual warfare? Do you think Satan is working more actively against you than you are working against him? Do you think your passive approach in spiritual warfare will be sufficient to fight him and his schemes? Take your stand! Walk in your authority. Fight with the authority that has been given you in Christ.

Like Jesus being tempted in the wilderness, we do not passively sit while the enemy assaults us. We stand against the enemy by the power of the Spirit and the truth of His Word. We use our God-given weapons to take our stand against all that is opposed to Christ (2 Cor. 10:4).

Just as a man must step in and intervene when he sees someone being physically assaulted, so a man must step in and intervene when he sees someone being spiritually assaulted. This means getting on our knees and praying, quoting Scripture, putting on the armor of God, resisting the devil, and standing against him.

My phone rang at 3:14 this morning. If you are a pastor, it's never good when your phone rings at 3:14 a.m. It was my daughter. She was at student camp. She woke up in the night with major anxiety, fear, nausea, and tremors. She was sick and scared. I'm 300 miles away. What can I do?

Well, among other things, I can get on my knees and stand against the enemy for her. That's not all I do, but that is one thing I *must* do. It's my right and responsibility.

Second, you express your authority by leading. Where do you lead? Go back to the chapter on assignments and look at the areas in which God has given you leadership. And in those areas, you take up the responsibility given to you, and you lead.

Nothing grieves me more than watching men fail to lead their wives and children. Before a man can effectively lead anyone or anything, he must first lead his family and his home. This is why, for a man to be a pastor, he must have shown that he can lead his family (Titus 1:6; 1 Tim. 3:5).

Men, pray with your wife. Initiate conversation. Deal with conflict. Make sure you don't go to bed angry. Lead out of your repentance, service, and humility.

Be the first one up on Sunday morning ensuring that your family goes to church. Make the hard decisions and tell your kids you will not let them sacrifice church for something of lesser importance. They don't make these decisions, you do. If you let your children make those decisions, you are giving away your authority.

The reason God gave children parents is that children are foolish and cannot raise themselves. They don't know what is right. As much as they think they know better, they simply don't. And they will test every fiber of your being. But your responsibility is to be their parent. If you will be faithful to be their parent when they are young, you will get to be their friend when they are older. But you are not called to win a popularity contest. You are called to lead, shepherd, guide, and instill wisdom into your children.

When a man fails to lead in his areas of responsibility, he is not only harming those under his charge; he is rebelling against the one who gave him those responsibilities. I know it gets tiring. I know it's challenging. I know it's complicated. But it's manhood. Make sure you are walking in your God-given authority as the leader God has called you to be, in every area God has assigned to you.

Finally, you express your authority by protecting. What should Adam have done when Satan approached his wife and began to lie to her? He should have taken his stand against the enemy on her behalf. He should have protected her. He should have sacrificed himself, if necessary, in order to protect her from the one who was trying to destroy her.

Fathers, you are called to protect your daughters from boys until they are ready to pursue a relationship that leads to marriage. You are called to protect their moral purity by not allowing them to dress immodestly. This is your job.

Fathers, you are called to protect your sons from foolishness by teaching them the way of wisdom and talking openly and honestly with them about the temptations they will face. As the father talks to his son in the book of Proverbs (chapters 1–9), we initiate conversations about the most serious issues in life.

I am continually amazed by the number of men who never have meaningful conversations with their sons about areas of moral purity, sexual temptation, the influence of friends, or the way to treat women with respect. God has not only given you the right to do those things; He has given you the *responsibility* to do those things. This kind of leadership in the life of your children is an expression of your God-given kingdom authority.

It is your job to protect your children against pornography and predators by not allowing them unmonitored access to phones. It is your job to protect your kids from foolish decisions by saying "no" to them. You are the protector. This is not just physical; it also refers to moral and spiritual protection.

You cannot stand aside when you see injustice. You cannot stand aside when you see someone under attack. Like Jesus, you must be willing to lay down your life for the good of others. God has given you a sword for a reason. You are a protector. And most of the time, that looks like being a deeply rooted man of God who stands in the gap for those under spiritual assault.

Don't forget, there is a lion on the loose, and he is after you and your family. Put up the proper protections. Take your stand. Don't let the lion prevail.

Remember This

I love parenting. I have four daughters, two of whom are teenagers right now. Honestly, I love being a dad to two teenage daughters. Parenting is one of the greatest joys of my life. I'm not just saying this—I would rather be home than any other place on earth. I love being with my kids.

But my wife and I often look at each other and say, "Parenting is a beating." I love it, but it is an unrelenting beating. It never stops and never gets easy.

Manhood is also a beating—never stopping and never getting easier. Learning to be a man who follows Jesus and embraces his God-given authority is hard. Passivity is so much easier. It's always easier to stay unengaged. It's always easier to remain quiet. It's always easier to let someone else raise your kids. It's always easier to ignore that the lion exists. It's always easier to just not decide. It's always easier to ignore the conflict. But the results are devastating.

Your failure to walk in your God-given kingdom authority will have devastating and eternal consequences. So embrace God's calling on your life, and don't give up. And remember, kingdom authority is about the right and responsibility to act and rule under the king, on behalf of the king, and for the king.

Finally, don't allow this to overwhelm you. Be encouraged. Being convicted of any area of deficiency is a work of grace in your life and gift from God. This is first and foremost about God calling you to live in submission to Him. Then, to allow His authority, filled with grace, kindness, and justice, to flow through you to others. This is a wonderful calling. So, take the next step. Whatever that might be. And pray that God would give you the grace to persevere.

Learning to be a man who follows Jesus and embraces his God-given authority is hard.

Discussion Questions

1. Initial thoughts . . . What resonates with you about this chapter? Is this idea new to you?

2. Can you think of any specific ways in which you have seen the negative effects of passivity from men?

3. In what areas do you tend to be the most passive? Why? What keeps you from leading the way you should?

4. Walking in authority means standing, leading, and protecting. In what specific areas do you need to walk in more authority?

Chapter 6

CHARACTER

MY DAD DIDN'T hunt, fish, camp, or work with wood. He didn't know how to skin a deer or fillet a fish. He couldn't tie a fly or catch trout. He knew nothing about guns or ammunition. He never rebuilt a transmission. He never owned a chain saw. I'm not even sure he could grow a good beard. Yet, I always saw my dad as a manly man.

My dad worked extremely hard. He had strong convictions. He never ran from a fight. He was a fierce protector. He was a sacrificial provider. And he was a man of great courage.

I didn't view my dad as a manly man because he possessed certain so-called manly skills; it was because he possessed a certain manly character. And to be clear, there *are* certain qualities associated with manliness. There always have been.

The apostle Paul ends his letter to the church in Corinth by saying, "Be watchful, stand firm in the faith, act like men, be strong" (1 Cor. 16:13). The phrase "act like men" could also be translated as "be courageous." Although this could be a call for every man and woman in the church to be courageous, this word in the original Greek meant "to behave like a man." Paul used this phrase because he believed there were certain qualities that were manly.

One of the greatest speeches ever recorded from a father to a son is the one David gave to Solomon in his dying days. David began his final words by saying, "I am about to go the way of the earth. Be strong, and show yourself a man" (1 Kings 2:2). David was calling his son Solomon to act in a distinctly manly way. He was calling him to be a man's man.

God calls every male to "act like a man." But this is not a call to embrace some kind of manly bravado or to learn certain manly skills. It does not refer to outward manly actions as much as it refers to an inward manly character.

E. M. Bounds said it this way:

> Conduct is what we do; character is what we are. Conduct is the outward life. Character is the life unseen, hidden within, yet evidenced by that which is seen. Conduct is external, seen from without; character is internal—operating within. In the economy of grace, conduct is the offspring of character. Character is the state of the heart, conduct its outward expression. Character is the root of the tree, conduct, the fruit it bears.[8]

When it comes to calling men into true manhood, there is a temptation to focus on the externals. Books and conferences for men tend to tell us that we must tap into our true inner outdoorsman to discover manhood. But a call to outward actions does not cultivate a man. A call to the cultivation of inner character makes a man. Therefore, the call to be a man is a call to apply great diligence to the cultivation of Christian character.

Character Is Cultivated

Our church has been working on a curriculum for children made up of five pillars every child needs to build a godly life. One of those pillars is the cultivation of virtues. We not only want to teach our children theological truths, Bible verses, prayer, and stories of God's faithfulness; we also want them to learn how to cultivate certain godly character qualities.

This conviction comes from verses like 2 Peter 1:5–8 which says,

> For this very reason, make every effort to supplement your faith with virtue, and virtue with knowledge, and knowledge with self-control, and self-control with steadfastness, and steadfastness with godliness, and godliness with brotherly affection, and brotherly affection with love. For if these qualities are

> yours and are increasing, they keep you from
> being ineffective or unfruitful in the knowl-
> edge of our Lord Jesus Christ.

God wants you to work hard to cultivate godly virtues. And since certain virtues are to be more distinctly manly, every man who chooses to follow Jesus must choose to work hard at cultivating these virtues. This is not something that happens by accident. This is something that happens when we apply "every effort."

I don't know why, but people tend to view Christian growth as unlike any other area of growth. A student knows that if he wants to do well on an exam, he doesn't just "let go and let God." He must study. A golfer does not get better by resting in his desire to be better. He practices. An entrepreneur does not succeed by sitting in his office dreaming of success. He works. But for some reason, we often think that growth in Christlikeness passively happens!

The Bible continually calls us to give our greatest effort to what is of greatest importance—namely, our relationship with Jesus Christ. In Philippians 2:12–13, Paul says it this way; "Therefore, my beloved, as you have always obeyed, so now, not only as in my presence but much more in my absence, work out your own salvation with fear and trembling, for it is God who works in you, both to will and to work for his good pleasure." In other words, believers must continue to work out what God continues to work in. We cannot "work in" our salvation. Only God can do that. But we must "work out" our salvation by applying great diligence. Our spiritual life is like any other area of our life—*growth demands effort.* Christian character does not appear out of nowhere or by chance; it is cultivated.

What Qualities Make a Man?

Paul left Titus in Crete to get the church in order (Titus 1:5). The first instruction in doing that was simple: "Appoint elders in every town." The greatest need in that highly dysfunctional church was godly men.

This church had men, but not the right kind. It was filled with "empty talkers and deceivers," "lazy gluttons," and men who were "detestable, disobedient, unfit for any good work." (1:10–16). Paul tells Titus exactly what kind of men he should look for:

> This is why I left you in Crete, so that you might put what remained into order, and appoint elders in every town as I directed you—if anyone is above reproach, the husband of one wife and his children are believers and not open to the charge of debauchery or insubordination. For an overseer, as God's steward, must be above reproach. He must not be arrogant or quick-tempered or a drunkard

or violent or greedy for gain, but hospitable, a lover of good, self-controlled, upright, holy, and disciplined. He must hold firm to the trustworthy word as taught, so that he may be able to instruct in sound doctrine and also to rebuke those who contradict it. (1:5–9)

Notice, when Paul told Titus to look for men to lead the church, he did not tell him to look primarily for intelligence, education, talent, or popularity. Paul told Titus to look for men of strong character. Paul told Timothy the same thing, and gave him a very similar list (1 Tim. 3:1–7). What makes this list so significant is that it gives us a clear paradigm of the kind of men we all should aspire to be, even if we don't aspire to become a pastor.

Gene Getz, in his classic book, *The Measure of a Man*, sees these two lists of qualifications of an elder as a guide for every man. He says, "While Paul was outlining criteria for selecting leaders, he was, in essence, saying, 'Timothy, if a man wants to become a spiritual leader, that's great. Just make sure he's a mature man, and here's how you can determine if he measures up to God's standards as a Christian. . . . The qualities, however, are goals for every Christian man."9

These two lists of qualities say to us, "Here is the kind of man God is looking for. This is what it means to be a man of character." Although 1 Timothy and Titus lay out twenty character qualities of a man of God, and each one deserves our prayerful attention and active cultivation, these qualities can be summarized in three broad categories: blamelessness, self-control, and courage.

Blamelessness

There is one overarching quality every man must cultivate. All other qualities flow from this one. It is so significant, that in Paul's list of qualifications for Titus, he mentions it twice. In a word, it is *blameless*.

Some versions translate this word as "above reproach," which might be a more helpful translation. The word does not mean "without blemish"; it means "without *blame*." We will only be without blemish when Christ completes His work in us and makes our salvation complete after death (Eph. 1:4; Col. 1:22).

To be blameless means to be a man of unquestionable integrity. It means you are not open to public attack or criticism. As has often been said, it means you are a man in whom no loophole for criticism can be found. It means you are a man who is a worthy model for other believers. It means you are the man in private whom you appear to be in public.

There are two primary areas in which we must seek to be blameless: at home and in the community.

Without any hesitation, Paul moves from the quality of blamelessness to a man's life at home. The probing question becomes, "Could your family share things about your life that would damage your reputation and disqualify you from leadership?"

This is when you kind of want to tell Paul to mind his own business.

Many churches will interview a man's wife before putting him in the office of deacon or pastor. The reason this is important is that there is one person who knows a man better than anyone else does, and that is his wife. This is also true of a man's children, and true of a younger man's parents.

Those closest to you are going to see the best and worst in you. Those closest to you will see your sin the most. They will see you when you are the most tired, grumpy, frustrated, and angry. No man is without fault at home. So, the issue is not that you are without any fault. The issue is how you respond when you are at fault at home.

A good friend of mine told me a story about his dad a few years ago that had a profound effect on me. My friend was at a county fair with his father when he was seven years old. He desperately wanted to ride the ponies, but the sign said that only kids six and under could ride. So, his father lied and told the operator his son was six so he could ride. My friend said that when he got off the ride, his dad's countenance was noticeably different, and he wasn't the same the rest of the day. Late that night, after my friend was in bed, his father came into his room, got on his knees, and while weeping, acknowledged to his son what he had done was sin and repented. That is what it means to be blameless at home.

Someone once said that being blameless at home is "righting your wrongs." You will do wrong. Over and over again. But the question is, do you make it right?

I want my kids to see me repent. I want them to see me weep over my sin. I want them to hear me say I'm sorry. They will never be able to say I am without blemish, but hopefully, through years of repentance and growth, they will say I am without blame.

You cultivate this quality by being quick to humbly repent when you are wrong. You cultivate it by asking those in your home to point out areas in which you need to improve. This is cultivated in the mundane moments as you seek to love and serve your family more. It is cultivated when you begin to see your home as the primary training ground for true manhood. It is cultivated when you seek to grow in your sacrificial, humble, Christ-centered love for your family and those around you.

Your blamelessness is also manifested in the community. Paul says that a man must not be "open to the charge of debauchery or insubordination" (Titus 1:6). The phrase "open to the charge" is significant. It means to be open to accusation. It asks the question, "Is there anyone out there with incriminating evidence against you?" Anyone in the workplace, in the community, or even online?

Imagine if we took an ad out in the newspaper and on social media with your name and picture with these words: "We are thinking about bringing this man into a position of leadership at our church. Does anyone in the community have any reason to think this would be a bad idea? Do you have any reason to think that having this man in a position of leadership in our church would hurt the reputation of Jesus Christ or our church?"

Would anyone at work respond? Anyone from the neighborhood, the golf course, or the little league? Would any woman bring up how you have talked to her or looked at her? Would anyone bring up your temper or language or attitude?

> The starting place for cultivating manly character is the pursuit of blamelessness.

The starting place for cultivating manly character is the pursuit of blamelessness. It is striving, by the power of the gospel of Jesus Christ, to live a life of integrity. It is a call to acknowledge your faults, say you're sorry, repent often, and make things right. It is a call to invite those closest to you to speak into your life and humbly receive what they say. It is a call to strive to live like a growing believer in the Lord Jesus Christ in every area of life—both public and private.

Self-Control

After laying the foundation of blamelessness, Paul gives a list of eleven qualities—five negatives, and six positives. You will notice they all demand a greater quality that is mentioned twice in Titus 1:8: "self-controlled" and "disciplined." In other words, you will never be a man of strong character unless you first be a man of strong self-discipline.

Just look at the five negative qualities Paul says destroy a man's character: arrogant, quick-tempered, drunkard, violent, and greedy for gain. Although each one of those deserves our careful consideration, the over-arching issue is the lack of self-control.

It is interesting that in the forty-six verses of the book of Titus, self-control is mentioned five times (1:8; 2:2; 2:5; 2:6; 2:12). You could make the case that self-control is one of the primary themes of the entire book. Paul knew the only way for this church to become healthy was for the members to cultivate self-control. This is true of every church and every family!

In chapter 2, as Titus receives specific instruction for each group in the church, he is commanded to teach the older men, older women, and younger men all to have self-control. But the most interesting mention of self-control is in Titus 2:6. After giving a series of instructions to older men and older women, Paul only gives *one admonition* to young men. He says, "Likewise, urge the young men to be self-controlled."

Is there anything a young man needs to learn more than self-control?

Here is the thing about self-control: if you don't learn it when you are a young man, you end up developing habits that affect you when you are an old man. Those areas in which you lacked self-control don't go away!

Over the past twenty years of pastoral ministry, I have learned a little principle: "Any area of a man's life that he does not get dominion over when he is young will get bigger, not better, the older he gets." The one message every young man needs to hear is this: learn to control your flesh while you are young, because if you don't, it will control you when you get older.

Self-control begets self-control. And, a lack of self-control begets more lack of self-control. What I mean is that to cultivate self-control, you must begin with the smaller areas of your life. Begin with a disciplined time with the Lord every day. Then gain control of your eating, commit to regular exercise, start coming home from work on time, and commit to consistent and personal time with your children.

> Learn to control your flesh while you are young, because if you don't, it will control you when you get older.

You cultivate discipline in the small areas of your life to become a disciplined, self-controlled person. There will be no growth in any area of Christian character if there is not the slow and steady cultivation of self-control.

Courage

Proverbs 28:1 says, "The wicked flee when no one pursues, but the righteous are bold as a lion." Over the years, this has become one of my favorite verses because I have seen the utter destruction of families, churches, and organizations brought on by passive men. My office is filled with pictures and little statues of lions as a constant reminder that the work God has called me to demands courage.

Many organizations, churches, families, and countries, have systemic problems that are all rooted in a man's lack of courage. If a man is not willing to do the hard things, make the hard decisions, and suffer for what is right, everyone around him suffers. Everyone suffers when men don't have courage.

I have prayed over the years that God would give me the courage to do what is right. The courage to stand. The courage to speak. The courage to act. God's calling in your life demands courage. And one of the greatest tools of the enemy, to hinder the work of the kingdom, is to get you to be passive. The enemy wants to trade a courageous heart with a quiet and cowardly heart. We must fight our tendency toward cowardice and passivity by cultivating a courageous heart.

When talking about spiritual warfare, a pastor friend of mine once said, "I don't see a demon behind every bush, but if it moves, I shoot it." Godly men aren't looking for a battle, but they are not afraid of a battle. Godly men know the effects of passivity are much more damaging than the cost of courage.

None of us are naturally courageous. In our flesh, we all tend to be like the cowardly lion in *The Wizard of Oz* who was scared of his own tail. Because true courage is not just the strength to do difficult things; it is the strength to do the right thing. It is the willingness to do the godly thing. True courage does not just take a stand; it takes a stand for godliness.

Psalm 31:24 says, "Be strong, and let your heart take courage, all you who wait for the LORD!" This verse reminds us that courage flows from confidence in the Lord. As our confidence in God increases, so does our courage. When a godly man acts with courage, it is because he is deeply rooted in the confidence of God.

As you walk with the Lord, you will not only grow in courage; you will grow in your ability to discern when that courage is needed. You will develop the depth of character that is needed to do what is right, no matter the cost. As your faith in God grows, so will your confidence.

Every assignment in your life demands courage, because every assignment in your life is hard. You will never use your plow and sword without courage. You will never live out your true identity nor walk in authority without courage. Courage is not an option; it is a necessity. A manly man is a courageous man.

Character Makes a Man

There seems to have been, among a previous generation of men, the belief that as long as a man provides for his family, he is being a man. As if the true test of manhood is a sufficient paycheck. No matter how else a man fails, if he provides for his children financially, he has fulfilled his responsibility.

I know this is still an issue because I meet with men all the time who believe this. Men who are far from being the kind of man God wants them to be. Men who are not growing in their self-sacrificial love for their families, their own self-control, or their courageous commitment to the things of the Lord, yet they feel like they are fine. They are satisfied. And most often, it's because they have believed the lie that as long as they bring home a paycheck, they are a manly man.

Most men have never been given a greater vision of what it means to be a man's man. This is why we need this instruction from Titus 1. Provision does not make a man. Character makes a man. And in the same way a man works hard to provide, he must work hard to cultivate character.

You were born a male, but you must grow into a man. The cultivation of character must become a constant, compelling, and lifelong commitment. And this commitment demands an active, daily pursuit of virtue. You must, like 2 Peter 1:5 says, "make every effort to supplement your faith with virtue."

Think about which virtues you need to cultivate most in your life. Ask those closest to you which areas they feel need the most improvement. Then take daily and practical steps to cultivating those virtues by the power of the Spirit.

> Provision does not make a man. Character makes a man.

If you are struggling with anger, confess that to the Lord and to those you have hurt; then begin to take practical steps to cultivate patience. If it is pride, cultivate humility. If it is lying, cultivate honesty. If it is irritation and irritability, cultivate consistency. If it is gluttony, cultivate self-control. If it is greed, cultivate generosity. No matter what the area of deficiency is, godly men work hard to cultivate godly character.

Don't continue to tolerate the areas in your life that are undermining the good work God is trying to do in and through you. In all of your other pursuits, don't forget the pursuit of character. If you do, at some point, everything else will crumble.

And remember, the goal is not just to be a good man. The goal is to be a godly man. The goal is to manifest the life of

Jesus Christ to everyone who is around you. And, you don't become like Jesus by passively hoping it happens. You seek to trust and follow Him every day, making the character of Jesus your greatest pursuit. You must cultivate your inner man, because your inner man is the man you really are.

Discussion Questions

1. What men in your life have demonstrated manly character? What have you learned from them?

2. As you look at the character qualities of a man in Titus 1, in which areas do you feel most deficient? Did the Lord convict you of anything specific?

3. In what specific ways can you cultivate those areas of character in which you need to grow?

4. Are there any sins, habits, or character deficiencies that you are tolerating instead of working to overcome?

Chapter 7

DOCTRINE

OVER THE PAST seven years, I have been involved in both leading and promoting church-wide discipleship groups. These are gender-specific groups of three to five that commit to read about one chapter of the Bible a day five days a week, keep some notes about their reading, and memorize one verse a week. These groups then meet weekly to discuss their reading, quote their verse, and keep each other accountable.

About halfway through each year, we gather all of our discipleship group leaders to see how they are doing, answer any questions, and encourage them to finish strong. Without exception, in every single leader meeting, every year, one question inevitably comes up. It is always from a male leader. And the question is always something like this: "I can't seem to get the guys in my group to keep up with their reading, and they say that they aren't good at memorizing verses. What should I do?"

I often hear a man tell me he's not good at memorizing and can't memorize a verse every week. Seriously? A second grader couldn't get away with a comment like that. And these are grown men. Many guys are investing very little time and effort into their spiritual life. And it is a sad and sobering indictment on the state of men in the church.

It grieves me at how far removed we have come from God's design and intention for men. God has designed men to be the primary leaders, teachers, and protectors of the faith, not only in the church, but in the home. And yet, we can't get many men to read one chapter of the Bible a day.

The book of Titus gives us a different vision for men—a vision of men who are deeply rooted in the Word of God and apply great effort to their knowledge of God. Men who understand the most important area of our life deserves the greatest effort of our life. Not just a little effort, but much effort.

Although this vision for men can be seen throughout the book of Titus, it is summarized in one primary verse. Titus 1:9 says, "He must hold firm to the trustworthy word as taught, so that he may be able to give instruction in sound doctrine and also to rebuke those who contradict it."

I realize this verse is for those aspiring to the office of an elder/pastor. But as we saw in the last chapter, these qualifications in Titus 1 and 1 Timothy 3 are to be a picture of the man God wants *every* man to be. Jonathan Edwards made the case that if God has called some men to be teachers, then He has called all men to be learners.[10] If the role of the pastor is to teach the Word, the role of the members is to learn.

God does not call every man to be a pastor, but He does call every man to be a learner. And these qualifications of a pastor remind us that being a godly man is not just about who we are, but what we know. Paul makes it clear he wants every man in the church to be sound in the faith (Titus 1:13). Titus gives us a fresh vision of what a godly man looks like—a vision of men deeply rooted in sound doctrine.

Men of Doctrine and Duty

When I first began using the book of Titus to raise up godly men in the church, I titled it "Titus 10: Men of Doctrine and Duty." I used that title because, after reading the forty-six verses of Titus over and over again, I could not think of a better phrase to describe the kind of men God wants us to be. This emphasis on both doctrine and duty is consistent from the beginning of the book to the end. Look at how often this is mentioned in Titus:

- Paul, a servant of God and an apostle of Jesus Christ, for the sake of the faith of God's elect and their knowledge of the truth, which accords with godliness (1:1).

- He must hold firm to the trustworthy word as taught, so that he may be able to give instruction in sound doctrine and also to rebuke those who contradict it (1:9).
- This testimony is true. Therefore rebuke them sharply, that they may be sound in the faith (1:13).
- But as for you, teach what accords with sound doctrine (2:1).
- Older men are to be sober-minded, dignified, self-controlled, sound in faith, in love, and in steadfastness (2:2).
- Show yourself in all respects to be a model of good works, and in your teaching show integrity, dignity, and sound speech that cannot be condemned, so that an opponent may be put to shame, having nothing evil to say about us (2:7–8).
- The saying is trustworthy, and I want you to insist on these things, so that those who have believed in God may be careful to devote themselves to good works. These things are excellent and profitable for people (3:8).

The relationship between right doctrine and right action is articulated over and over. Paul says that his motive for writing this letter in the first place was to instruct people in the kind of knowledge that leads to godliness (1:1). He is writing because the church is filled with men who say they know the truth, but deny it by their actions. He says these men are "detestable, disobedient, unfit for any good work" (1:16). Their lack of godliness is rooted in their lack of knowledge of the truth.

There seems to be this idea that sound doctrine and aggressive action are in opposition to one another. As if some men study and some men work. I feel this at times in the church. People will say things like, "We need less Bible studies and more action!" I understand the sentiment. We have way too many believers who attend every Bible study the church offers but ignore the calls for service or evangelism. But Paul's vision is a study of doctrine that fuels passionate action. Sound doctrine and fruitful action are not in opposition to each other. Sound doctrine is intended to be the foundation for fruitful action.

> Sound doctrine is intended to be the foundation for fruitful action.

There is no virtue in ignorance. We should never settle for having a mind that is not filled with what is most important. If God is of greatest value, He deserves our greatest thought.

Rooted

I am currently leading a discipleship group with four, eighth-grade guys. I love those young men. They encourage me in countless ways. For about a month, our memory verse had us memorizing all of Psalm 1. I've memorized Psalm 1 a few times over the past thirty years, but this time it was more meaningful to me than ever. At this stage in my life, I love the idea of being a deeply rooted tree, bearing fruit, and not withering. I'm not sure there is anything I want in my life at this moment more than I want to be rooted.

The idea of being "rooted" like an old oak tree is essential in the pursuit of godliness. One of Paul's most frequent exhortations is to "stand firm in the faith." First Corinthians 16:13 says, "Be watchful, stand firm in the faith, act like men, be strong." Paul gives this call in almost every letter he writes. A man can only stand firm when he is deeply rooted.

How do we become deeply rooted? According to Psalm 1, it is by delighting in the law of the Lord and meditating on it day and night. We are deeply rooted through years of consistent meditation, memorization, reading, and study of God's Word. A man who is unwilling to read a chapter a day and memorize a verse a week will never be deeply rooted in the faith.

Don't you want to be "like a tree, planted by streams of water, that yields its fruit in season, and its leaf does not wither? In all that he does, he prospers" (v. 3)? I can't imagine anything better. And you can be that man. But it demands a life committed to God's Word.

Sound Doctrine

When Paul tells Titus to look for men who "hold firm to the trustworthy word, so that he may be able to instruct in sound doctrine and also to rebuke those who contradict it" (Titus 1:9), he is telling Titus to look for men who are deeply rooted in sound doctrine. Sound doctrine is the roots.

But what exactly *is* sound doctrine?

When Paul talks about "doctrine" he is referring to the truth God has revealed about Himself. Where "trustworthy words" might refer to God's revelation in His Word, "doctrine" would refer to the specific truths contained in the Word. For example, if you were to buy a book on basic Bible doctrines, you would find topics such as the Bible, God, mankind, salvation, and the church. These chapters would be a summary of what the Bible as a whole says about those specific topics. Doctrine is truth.

The word *sound* means healthy. To have "sound doctrine" means you have doctrine that leads to life. Doctrine that heals, nurtures, and feeds. The vision for manhood here is that every man seeks not only to read and understand the Bible but to have a good working knowledge of the major truths of God's Word. The kind of knowledge that heals, nurtures, and feeds those under his care. This is part of taking dominion. Being rooted in sound doctrine is essential to fulfilling your role as a man.

This admonition is a call to take seriously that which is most serious—namely, God and the truth about Him. This is a call to seek for Him like silver and search for Him like a hidden treasure (Prov. 2:4). That you would not settle for a surface understanding of God but would seek to know that doctrine which leads to godliness.

The Implications of Ignorance

I had only been a pastor for a few months when a young man who grew up in the church asked to have lunch with me. He wanted to talk about his relationship with a girl he was planning to marry. I asked this young man if this girl was a Christian. He responded, "Well, she comes from a good family and she seems to do a lot of good things. So, I think so."

This is a young man who grew up in the church. He attended church for five years of pre-school, six years of

children's ministry, and seven years of student ministry. And
this was a good church. Yet, after eighteen years in a Bible-
believing, Bible-preaching church, he thought his girlfriend
was a Christian because she "did a lot of good things."

I have been haunted by that conversation for more than
fifteen years. His complete lack of understanding regarding
the gospel is not just tragic; it is terrifying and eternally
condemning.

I don't put all the responsibility on the church. It is
primarily the parents' responsibility to teach and train their
children the things of the Lord and ensure they understand
the gospel. But how does this young man spend eighteen years
in a church and not understand the most basic message of the
church? It's not that he understood it and chose not to believe
it. It's that he didn't have the basic understanding one could
get from a simple gospel tract. You cannot tell me that doctrine does not matter.

Lack of care and concern about doctrine has massive and
eternal consequences. This is the entire reason Paul left Titus
in Crete. The church in Crete was being ravaged by false
teachers. Listen to what Paul says about them:

> For there are many who are insubordinate,
> empty talkers and deceivers, especially those
> of the circumcision party. They must be
> silenced, since they are upsetting whole fami-
> lies by teaching for shameful gain what they

ought not to teach. One of the Cretans, a prophet of their own, said, "Cretans are always liars, evil beasts, lazy gluttons." This testimony is true. Therefore rebuke them sharply, that they may be sound in the faith, not devoting themselves to Jewish myths and the commands of people who turn away from the truth. To the pure, all things are pure, but to the defiled and unbelieving, nothing is pure; but both their minds and their consciences are defiled. They profess to know God, but they deny him by their works. They are detestable, disobedient, unfit for any good work. (Titus 1:10–16)

The church was being destroyed, families were being torn apart, the name of God was being shamed in the community—all because of false doctrine. And specifically, by men who did not have a proper understanding of the gospel!

If we want to be men of God, we must be men of truth. Men who are deeply rooted and grounded in the things of the Lord.

Satan is a liar. Ignorance and false teaching are the names of his game. It is a very effective

> If we want to be men of God, we must be men of truth.

tactic. He leads millions astray with those weapons every day. But Jesus has come to deliver us from Satan's lies by giving us the truth and declaring the truth will make us free (John 14:6; 8:32). The truth matters. And ignorance has consequences. God's vision for you is that you be deeply rooted, firm in the faith, sound in doctrine.

Why You Need Doctrine

When I titled this chapter "Doctrine," my first thought was that men would skip it. Honestly.

I was afraid men would look at the word and immediately think it wasn't for them. But I hope you see when we talk about doctrine, we are talking about *knowing God*. We're talking about being a sound, solid, rooted man who not only knows the truths of God, but is able to teach them to others.

This matters more than you think. Let's look at four primary reasons you need doctrine.

To Understand the Gospel

First, you need doctrine because you need to understand the gospel. Is anything more important than this? Not only for yourself but all those God has placed under your influence. The gospel is both incredibly simple and profoundly deep. Just think about that in terms of Titus 2.

For the grace of God has appeared, bringing salvation for all people, training us to renounce ungodliness and worldly passions, and to live self-controlled, upright, and godly lives in the present age, waiting for our blessed hope, the appearing of the glory of our great God and Savior Jesus Christ, who gave himself for us to redeem us from all lawlessness and to purify for himself a people for his own possession who are zealous for good works. Declare these things; exhort and rebuke with all authority. Let no one disregard you. (vv. 11–15)

This message is simple. God sent His Son into this world to save sinners. But there is so much beauty and glory and life-forming truth in this summary of the gospel: seeing Jesus as the appearing of God's grace; understanding how the gospel not only saves us, but trains us; knowing the hope that awaits us when Jesus returns; feeling the weight, cost, and joy of redemption; realizing that God is gathering for Himself a distinct people who manifest His glory through their good works. These are incredible truths!

And remember, the theological issues in the church in Crete—those issues that were tearing apart families—were all issues about the gospel. Men who misunderstood the gospel were destroying the church.

Please don't be satisfied with enough knowledge of the gospel to get you to heaven. Seek to understand the gospel in its fullness. The gospel does not just save us; the gospel changes us and forms us and empowers us and infuses us with hope for today. You need the gospel every moment. You need to swim in the depths of it and let it constantly change you. That is what doctrine is for.

> You need the gospel every moment.

To Understand the Bible

Second, you need to understand the Bible. It wasn't until after attending a Christian university, being a full-time missionary, and completing three years of theological education, that I began to understand the whole story line of the Bible. And when I saw it, it changed everything.

I was communicating this to my pastoral staff recently, and three other pastors said they had the same experience. Once they saw the Bible as one united story—and at the center of that story was God's plan to save His people by the sacrifice of His Son—every other story in the Bible began to make sense. I'm not sure why it took all of us so long to see this, but I think it's because most of us didn't grow up in churches that clearly taught it.

If you do not understand the basic storyline of the Bible, you will misunderstand, misinterpret, and frankly be confused by so much of it. You need to learn the basic story line of Scripture so you can rightly understand and communicate God's Word. That is what doctrine is for.

To Teach the Word

Third, you need to be able to teach the Word. In some form or fashion, every believer is called on to teach the Word. Most will never do it formally, but everyone will do it. You teach the Word when you share the gospel with an unbeliever. You teach the Word when you get into a discussion about creation, sexuality, ethics, or marriage. You teach the Word when a coworker, classmate, or friend asks you any question about God. You teach the Word when you lead your family in devotions.

This is certainly true for fathers. The primary place for theological instruction is in the home (Deuteronomy 6). This means every father must know how to teach the Word. You learn to understand and teach the Word as you choose to dive a little deeper into the basic truths of the Word—first for the sake of your own relationship with the Lord, and then for the sake of everyone around you, especially those under your authority. That is what doctrine is for.

To Guard the Truth

Finally, you need to be able to guard the truth. I don't think I need to waste time convincing you that all of our basic

Christian truths are under attack. I know enough history to know we are not living in the evilest days ever, but I do know we are living in complicated times in which the truths we hold dear are being constantly questioned.

Every day the truth is challenged. Every day lies are being told. But this doesn't just come in the obvious ways. We know Satan is like a prowling lion, looking to devour believers (1 Pet. 5:8). We know he's the father of lies (John 8:44). But we should also remember that he comes disguised as an angel of light (2 Cor. 11:14). Satan is far too crafty to come at us only through a full-frontal attack; like he did with Eve, he comes with subtlety, deception, and cleverness. He offers us what looks good. And in doing so, he undermines the truth. Only if we are intimately acquainted with truth can we recognize its counterfeit. Only when you know sound doctrine will you recognize Satan's lies.

As much as we need to know the basic doctrines of Scripture, in the times in which we live, being able to communicate the basic truths is not really enough. We need to know how to engage in conversations about sexual ethics, the sanctity of marriage and human life, and discerning truth from lies. I read an article recently about sixty-five questions every parent needs to be able to answer. At first, sixty-five questions seemed like a bit of a stretch. But as I read the questions, I realized every one of these questions is faced by normal teenagers today. And I couldn't help but wonder how many men were equipped to have these conversations.

This is not just about a head full of knowledge. Our ability to teach and instruct others is a matter of life and death. If the enemy's greatest tactic is lies, we must be able to confront them with truth.

Has there ever been a time with a greater need than for men to guard, protect, and stand for the truth? That is what doctrine is for.

Becoming Sound in Doctrine

I love when I see men in my church take doctrine seriously. This is because I believe that the Spirit-filled study of doctrine will lead those men to be stronger and more active in the work of the Lord. I love seeing men take the Bible seriously. I love seeing men choose to develop and cultivate a strong mind that can stand for the truths our ancestors died to protect. But the question is, how do you begin to make progress in understanding doctrine?

It begins with desire. You will never pursue something you do not desire. Listen to what Solomon says about the desire for truth:

> Blessed is the one who finds wisdom, and
> the one who gets understanding, for the gain
> from her is better than gain from silver and

her profit better than gold. She is more precious than jewels, and nothing you desire can compare with her. Long life is in her right hand; in her left hand are riches and honor. Her ways are ways of pleasantness, and all her paths are peace. She is a tree of life to those who lay hold of her; those who hold her fast are called blessed. (Prov. 3:13–18)

What could you desire that compares to the knowledge of God? Nothing. Nothing you desire compares. Some of you already desire it. Praise the Lord. If you don't, pray for it. Desire comes from God. God will give it to you if you ask Him for it. Ask God to give you a passion and longing for truth.

Desire then must lead to discipline. We discipline ourselves for godliness. There is no growth in any area of life without discipline. Desiring to lose weight has never made anyone skinny. Losing weight must begin with desire, but it cannot end there. That desire must lead to discipline. So it is with our desire for truth. The desire must manifest itself in a life that makes truth a priority (1 Tim. 4:7–8).

This begins, without question, with a commitment to regular Bible reading. Don't run to theology books. Run to the Bible. No area of our life will grow unless we are committed to regular time in God's Word. Start with a chapter a day, but don't stop there. Consume the Word. Treat it like the treasure it is. Go after it.

Apart from desire and discipline, here are some other practical tips:

- *Buy a good study Bible.* Don't let the notes in the Bible take the place of reading the Bible, but begin to read the notes as you have questions or get tripped up in your Bible reading. Seek to gain more understanding from the passages you are already reading. This is a great place to start.

- *Focus on one book of the Bible for a while.* For a season, instead of trying to check off all the boxes on your Bible reading plan, plant yourself in one book for an extended period of time. Read it over and over again. Look for keywords and themes.

- *Use a good commentary.* If you are reading one specific book of the Bible, find one good commentary that you can turn to for help and insight. Ask your pastor for recommendations, because there are lots of commentaries out there!

- *Read a book on the story line of the Bible.* There are many good resources out there.

God's Big Picture by Vaughan Roberts and *Gospel and Kingdom* by Graeme Goldsworthy were the first books that opened my eyes to this idea.

- *Start a book study.* Gather a group of men every week and read through a systematic theology or a book on a specific doctrine.
- *Study a statement of faith.* My specific denomination has a solid statement of faith which is a great place to begin learning the basic doctrines. There are also many historic statements of faith (often called "confessions of faith") like the New Hampshire Confession of Faith or the Apostles' Creed.
- *Learn a catechism.* This might sound archaic, but the most helpful thing you could do to learn and teach others the most basic truths of Scripture is to learn a catechism. Catechisms were written specifically to teach children and adults doctrine by communicating them in question-and-answer form. There are many historic catechisms as well as new ones, like the one from the Gospel Project.

Don't Act like a Brute

About twenty years ago I read a sermon by Jonathan Edwards on Hebrews 5:12, titled "Christian Knowledge." Not only have I continued to reflect on the words from this sermon, but I have also used them over and over to encourage people to give more time to studying God's Word. You should read it. Trying to summarize it seems cheap. But let me try.

Edwards makes the case that the primary thing distinguishing us from the brutes (meaning, animals) is our ability to reason. And God has given us the ability to reason primarily so we would think about and understand the things of the Lord. When we fail to use our ability to reason to think about the Lord, and instead just use the senses and appetites we have in common with the brutes, we essentially bring ourselves down to the level of the brutes. When we fail to think deeply about the Lord, we not only fail to behave like Christians, we forget we are men and act like brutes.

To put this in my own words—if you fail to use your mind to think about the things of the Lord, you're just acting like an animal. So, don't act like an animal. Be a deeply rooted man, sound in doctrine.

Discussion Questions

1. Why is doctrine essential to your calling as a man? Be specific. How does the lack of doctrine effect you?

2. Are you spending regular time seeking to know God and His word better? Honestly. Why or why not?

3. What are your hindrances to growth in doctrine?

4. What specific steps will you take to begin to grow in doctrine?

Chapter 8

MISSION

YOU WERE CREATED for a mission. It's in your DNA. Every man has something in him that wants to attempt great things, accomplish great things, and be a part of great things. There is, in the heart of every man, even if he has never identified it, a desire to be a part of something greater than himself.

Men long for a fight. Men want to be a part of a battle. Men want to stand for justice and make wrong things right. Men are naturally allergic to boredom. And this desire for a mission has led mankind to do some incredible things.

This is not just anecdotal. It's also not just a sociological observation about what makes men tick or what satisfies a man's urge for adventure. Men were created for a mission. Men must have a mission to fulfill. Without some grand, life-consuming mission, you will never feel as if your life matters.

Without a compelling mission, men respond in different ways. Some settle for a life filled with mediocrity and the mundane, assuming they just need to bury their boyish dreams and ambitions. Others become desperately bored and, in an attempt to find something more exciting in life, make foolish decisions. Others will be driven by a constant sense of dissatisfaction, causing them always to leave what they currently have in a desperate search for something better— something more exciting.

In simplistic terms, isn't this the source of most midlife crises? There is a stage in a man's life when he wakes up and thinks, *Is this it? Is this as good as it's going to get? Wasn't life supposed to be more exciting than this?* Those questions lead men into feelings of boredom, emptiness, and rebellion. So, without any greater mission, they turn back into rebellious teenagers and make stupid and damaging decisions.

Men without a mission are dangerous to themselves and everyone around them. Men must have a mission. If this desire for a mission is not properly discovered, cultivated, and empowered, the results can be catastrophic. This is why every man must understand his own role in the mission of God.

> Men without a mission are dangerous.

The Mission of God

You were created for a mission because you were created in the image of a missionary God. God has always had a mission. It has often been said, "God did not create a mission for His people; He created a people for His mission." This is true. God did not create mankind and then realize they would be bored if He didn't give them something to do. God created mankind to fulfill His mission. Before mankind ever existed, God had a mission.

We see the mission of God in the garden of Eden before sin even entered the picture. Eden was the place of God's presence. Eden was the temple of God. Adam and Eve found their complete fulfillment in Eden because God was there, walking among them (Gen. 3:8). This is a picture of life as it was meant to be.

True life is always found in the presence of God. It is in God's presence that you come to understand what you were created for. It is in God's presence that you come to know true life. It is in God's presence where every desire of your heart is fulfilled. You exist for His presence and only discover life in His presence. Everything flows from the presence of God (Pss. 16; 36). This is why you must continually seek the presence of God and continually have your soul satisfied in God (Pss. 27:8; 42:1).

The presence of God in Eden is symbolized by the river flowing out of Eden. Genesis 2:10 says, "A river flowed out of

Eden to water the garden, and there it divided and became four rivers." The river flowing out of Eden symbolizes the very presence of God giving life to everything in Eden. But there was more than one river in Eden.

The river flowing out of Eden divided into four different rivers. If the river flowing into Eden represents the presence of God bringing life to Eden, the four rivers flowing out of Eden represent the presence of God flowing out of Eden, bringing life to the nations.[11]

And this is the heart of God. God has created all of mankind to be truly satisfied only in His presence. As Augustine of Hippo famously said, "Thou hast made us for thyself, O Lord, and our heart is restless until it finds its rest in thee."[12] Because we were created for God, and will only find satisfaction in God, God desires to spread His presence to the ends of the earth. This is why four rivers are leaving Eden and going to the nations.

Habakkuk communicated this vision when he said, "For the earth will be filled with the knowledge of the glory of the LORD as the waters cover the sea" (Hab. 2:14). This is the longing of the psalmist when he says, "Declare his glory among the nations, his marvelous works among all the peoples!" (Ps. 96:3). This is the passion of Isaiah when he says, "Sing to the LORD a new song, his praise from the end of the earth" (Isa. 42:10). The heart-cry of God, and those who embrace the heart of God—that every person might come to know the satisfying reality of God's presence.

God's mission has always been that all people know and worship Him. John Piper says it this way:

> Missions is not the ultimate goal of the church. Worship is. Missions exists because worship doesn't. Worship is ultimate, not missions, because God is ultimate, not man. . . . Worship, therefore, is the fuel and goal of missions. It's the goal of missions because in missions we simply aim to bring the nations into the white-hot enjoyment of God's glory. The goal of missions is the gladness of the peoples in the greatness of God.[13]

If it is only in the presence of God that people find life, joy, satisfaction, purpose, and fulfillment, the greatest demonstration of God's love would be to call all people to come into His presence, through Jesus Christ, and worship Him. This is the mission of God. This is the mission you were created for.

An Important Transition

For a man to join in the mission of God, there is an important transition that must happen in his life. It is a transition seen in the book of Titus.

The first chapter of Titus focuses on the inner workings of the church—specifically, on the primary need for godly men to step into leadership. Chapter 2 of Titus moves from the leaders to the congregation. A church not only needs godly men and women. But for the first time in this little book, chapter 3 moves from life inside the church to life outside the church. And this is the transition that every man must make.

The local church is at the center of God's mission. God intends to accomplish His mission through the local church. As we have talked about at length, the local church must be a priority in the life of every man. A man will never be on a mission with God unless he is connected to a local church. But the goal is not just well-functioning, properly led, healthy churches. The goal is well-functioning, properly led, healthy churches that engage in the mission of God.

Many good men have failed to make the transition from life inside the church to life outside the church. There are so many men in the church who love the Bible, love preaching, love leadership, and even love serving, but have never fully embraced the mission of God. They have made the means the end. Instead of seeing the local church as the means by which God intends to reach the nations, they have made the church the end. Instead of seeing the church as the launching point, the church has become the landing pad. This transition to life outside the church, life on mission with God, a life consumed with spreading the glory of Christ to the ends of the earth, is a transition that must take place in your heart.

It is appropriate that Titus 3, the chapter that makes the transition from life inside the church to life outside the church, begins with the words "Remind them." Paul tells Timothy to "remind them" because this was something they already knew. Yet, of all things, Paul knew that this was something they needed to hear again.

For some reason, this is always the case when it comes to a life on mission. Every man of God knows He is called to be on a mission. Most can quote the Great Commission and even give the reference. Yet, this one area demands constant reminding. Our problem is not that we don't know we should do it; our problem is that we just don't do it. And if we are not careful, every man, even the greatest of men, will begin to settle for a life of ministry within the church without engaging in a life of mission outside the church.

We cannot fail to make this important transition. You must be constantly reminded that you were created for a mission.

Saved From and Saved For

Every man of God not only needs to be regularly reminded of the mission; he also needs to be regularly reminded of the gospel. It is through continually hearing the gospel that we are reminded that God not only saved us *from* something; God also saved us *for* something.

> Remind them to be submissive to rulers and authorities, to be obedient, to be ready for every good work, to speak evil of no one, to avoid quarreling, to be gentle, and to show perfect courtesy toward all people. For we ourselves were once foolish, disobedient, led astray, slaves to various passions and pleasures, passing our days in malice and envy, hated by others and hating one another. But when the goodness and loving kindness of God our Savior appeared, he saved us, not because of works done by us in righteousness, but according to his own mercy, by the washing of regeneration and renewal of the Holy Spirit, whom he poured out on us richly through Jesus Christ our Savior, so that being justified by his grace we might become heirs according to the hope of eternal life. The saying is trustworthy, and I want you to insist on these things, so that those who have believed in God may be careful to devote themselves to good works. These things are excellent and profitable for people. (Titus 3:1–8)

The first word of the second sentence is significant: *For.* The reason you need to honor your employer, be obedient to authorities, be ready to show every good work, speak in a way that is honoring to the Lord, be gentle, and show courtesy to all people is that you have been saved!

Before you gave your life to Christ, you were foolish, disobedient, led astray, and slaves to your passions. Before Jesus, you passed your days with evil and hatred. But when Jesus appeared, He saved you from all of that. He delivered you through His death and changed you through regeneration. He made you into a new creation. You were born again. God has saved you from a meaningless and broken life.

But you have not only been saved from something; you have also been saved for something. You must continually hear the gospel in your own life so you might in turn be careful to devote yourself to good works. Paul tells Titus to keep preaching the gospel to believers. Keep insisting on how they should live. Why? Because the continual preaching of the gospel is a constant reminder that you were saved from sin and for a mission.

So many men seem to think the gospel is just a message of being saved from sin. The result is, they want to "accept Jesus" and then continue in their same way of living. And then they

> Many men seem to think the gospel is just a message of being saved from sin.

wonder why following Jesus is not fulfilling! Someone who "accepts Jesus" and continues in his old life, might have "accepted" something, but he is not a follower of Jesus Christ. A true follower of Jesus Christ is someone who believes Jesus is the way, and in response, follows Jesus on the way. Salvation is being saved from sin and being saved for new life. The gospel gives you a mission.

The Mission of Man

When Jesus called His disciples, He did so with two words: "Follow me" (Luke 5:27). It was a call both to trust and follow Jesus. The very act of leaving everything behind and following Jesus was an act of faith. In order to follow Him, they had to believe Jesus knew where He was going and was worth following.

The disciples had no idea of the adventure that awaited them when they accepted that invitation. In the following days, weeks, months, and years, they would see Jesus heal the sick, calm storms, cast out demons, raise the dead, preach to multitudes, and publicly expose the religious Pharisees of the day. They would not only see His actions, but they would also hear His words and come to know His heart. If any man thinks following Jesus is boring and unengaging, it is because he is not following Jesus.

When talking about hiring staff, my father would always say, "A man cannot reproduce what he has not experienced." I have found that to be true. Before the disciples could reproduce it, they had to see it. And they did. In miraculous ways. But then, Jesus quickly called them to reproduce it.

In Luke 9, Jesus called His disciples together, gave them power and authority, and sent them out to proclaim the kingdom of God and to heal. He told them to take nothing with them—nothing but power and authority. Jesus didn't give them much more instruction. He didn't need to. They had seen it. Jesus simply sent them out to do what they had watched him do.

When we come to the Great Commission passages (Matt. 28:18–20; Mark 16:15; Luke 24:44–49; John 20:21; Acts 1:8), we get the same feeling. People spend so much time trying to evaluate and understand these passages, when in reality, Jesus is looking at His disciples and saying, "Go do for others what I did for you." The simplicity of the Commission is summarized in Jesus's words in John 20:21, when He says, "As the Father has sent me, even so I am sending you."

In other words, God is calling you to trust and follow Jesus, and as you discover what this means in your own life, you then reproduce that.

We can summarize the Great Commission passages with these words: lead people to trust and follow Jesus. This is what Jesus did, and this is, in the simplest terms, what Jesus is calling us to do. The phrase "leading people to trust and follow Jesus" includes everything in Matthew 28:18–20. We begin by calling people to trust and follow Jesus through the proclamation of the gospel. As they receive that invitation, we baptize them as a public profession of their faith. Then we continue to call them to trust and follow Jesus through the ongoing teaching of God's Word.

The call to trust and follow Jesus is not a one-time summons; it is the calling of the everyday life of every believer in Jesus Christ.

The mission of man is the mission we see manifested in the life and ministry of Jesus. As the Father sent Jesus, He is sending you. He sends you out into everyday life to be humble, sacrificial, Spirit-filled ambassadors who spread the glory of God and call people to worship Him.

Declaring and Displaying

If your model for mission is found in the model of Jesus, then your mission must include both declaring and displaying the gospel. When Jesus preached, "The kingdom of God is at hand" (Mark 1:15), He went on both to declare and display the kingdom.

When the crowds searched for Him in the early morning and found Him in a desolate place spending time with His Father, they begged Him to stay with them. But He said, "I must preach the good news of the kingdom of God to other towns as well; for I was sent for this purpose" (Luke 4:43). Jesus had to preach because the gospel was news that had to be declared.

Yet, everywhere He went, He displayed the gospel of the kingdom. When He healed the sick, delivered people from demonic spirits, fed the multitudes, and ate in the homes of religious leaders and sinners, He was displaying the kingdom. Each of these things was a little picture of the kingdom that was to come.

The way we engage with God in His mission is still the same. We join God in His mission by declaring and displaying the gospel of the kingdom.

The gospel must be declared. We must embrace our responsibility to share verbally the good news of Jesus Christ. People will not be saved unless they hear the truths about God, man, Jesus, and the way to trust and follow Him (refer back to the fuller explanation of the gospel in chapter 2). You may do this at one time or over the course of several conversations. *But people must hear the gospel.*

> We join God in His mission by declaring and displaying the gospel of the kingdom.

Verbally sharing the gospel seems to be the most difficult thing for almost every man. It is for me. And I'm not exactly sure why. I think some of it has to do with the fear of man. I think some of it has to do with a sense of inadequacy or the fear we might be asked a question we can't answer. But I think most of it is spiritual warfare. The enemy does not want us to communicate the gospel verbally, so he fights against every instinct we have to be obedient in this area.

For generations, pastors have begged their men to share the gospel and continually made them feel guilty for not doing it. But I believe the biggest battle in getting men to share the gospel is the spiritual battle every man must fight for himself—the battle against the enemy who wants to make every man ineffective in his mission. The battle against fear, anxiety, insecurity, and all the other lies the enemy whispers in our ear.

For a man to be someone who faithfully declares the gospel, he must take his stand against the enemy, fight off all the ungodly and unfounded fears, and courageously open his mouth out of sheer obedience to the call of Jesus Christ.

But the gospel must not only be declared; it must be displayed. That is the point of Titus 3:1–2: "Remind them to be submissive to rulers and authorities, to be obedient, to be ready for every good work, to speak evil of no one, to avoid quarreling, to be gentle, and to show perfect courtesy toward all people." These verses are a sobering reminder that our outward actions have a massive impact on the fulfillment of our mission. Our mission is not just to speak; our mission is to live.

Do you realize that part of your mission is fulfilled in the way you treat your boss? It is fulfilled in the way you talk to people at work, the way you work, and the way you treat those you don't necessarily like.

I had a man come to my office a few years back because he was disturbed by some comments I made regarding Muslims. Specifically, my calls for the church to love Muslims. He wanted to make sure I knew the truths about Muslims and their "agenda to take over America." I listened to everything he had to say. And then, I just asked him to read Titus 3:2 and tell me how he should respond to a Muslim when he sees one. What does it mean to "show perfect courtesy to everyone"? At the very least, it means going out of our way to show kindness to every single person we come in contact with. Including Muslims, and people of all different religions and worldviews.

Just imagine the power and influence of your life if you just took that one phrase seriously. Imagine the impact you would make if your life is marked by "perfect courtesy." If you just took that one phrase this week and, by the power of the Holy Spirit, tried to make it a reality in your life every day, you would be displaying the gospel in a way most people have never seen. "Perfect courtesy" is almost nonexistent in our culture. Someone who displayed it would be noticeable and powerful.

God did not just save you so you would attend church and act nice when you get there. God saved you to transform you. And He intended for that inner transformation to be manifested in your outward actions. He saved you so that every moment of your life would feel significant, because every moment of your life is a part of the mission of God.

Every Neighbor, Every Nation

Just recently the Lord has captured my heart with one phrase: *every neighbor, every nation.* This simple phrase provides a compelling and practical vision for the mission of God.

Your neighbor is not just the person next door. Jesus says your neighbor is everyone you come in contact with—especially those you might be most inclined to neglect or dislike (Luke 10). Your neighbor is anyone you are in proximity to. Anyone you work with, live near, go to school with, or pass on the street. God's mission always begins with our neighbor.

I once had a church member ask me if I would come to their house and share the gospel with their neighbor. I politely declined. I told them that I had my own neighbors to share the gospel with!

It's not the pastor's job to share the gospel with your neighbor; it's yours.

Many years ago, Oscar Thompson wrote a book titled *Concentric Circles of Concern.* He made the point that the gospel moves primarily through relationships. These concentric relational circles move out from our self, to our family, to our relatives, to our friends, to our neighbors, to our acquaintances, all the way to people we meet but do not know. These are to be our circles of concern. He then said that God holds every person accountable for the people He brings into their sphere of influence.

Our missionary assignment begins with our neighbors, but our vision is not just reaching every *neighbor*; our vision is reaching every *nation* for Christ. Our vision must contain every nation because God's mission contains every nation. His goal has always been that the nations know and rejoice in Him (Ps. 67).

At the time of writing this book, there are 7,402 unreached people groups in the world. A people group is a community that shares an ethnicity and a language. A people group is considered "unreached" when less than 2 percent of its population is Christian. The total population of those people groups is 3.27 billion. Unreached people groups make up 42.2 percent of the world's population.

Of those unreached people groups, there are 3,150 who are considered Unengaged Unreached People Groups. Those are groups that have no Christian presence and have no known church planting activity underway.

It is estimated that more than 66,000 people die every day without having *any access* to the gospel.[14]

In college, I had a professor who said the word *go* in the Great Commission meant "as you go." He then said our responsibility is to reach those we come in contact with as we go through life. Here is the massive problem with that: *unengaged and unreached people groups are not on the way for anyone.* These remaining unengaged people groups are often in remote and dangerous locations.

Our church is currently trying to reach an unengaged and unreached people group called the Naaba people in a remote area of Nepal. They are a Himalayan people who live in remote villages. To reach them, our teams must take a 26-hour flight from Atlanta to Kathmandu. They then take a 35-minute flight on a small plane to the city of Tumlingar. Once there, they ride a jeep for four hours, and then trek on foot for three days.

If the Great Commission is just a call to reach people on your way, the Naaba people will never hear the gospel.

You must begin with every neighbor. You don't have to wait for that. Right now, God is calling you to step into His mission by declaring and displaying the gospel to those around you. And as you step out in faith and engage in His mission to your neighbors, He will cultivate in you an increasing passion to see more people come to Christ. You will not only long to see your neighbors come to Christ, but you will also begin to feel a burden for the nations. And the ultimate goal of joining God's mission is making this the greatest aim of our life until every neighbor and every nation hears the glorious news of Jesus Christ.

Fueling the Fire

Three months after graduating from college, I moved to Slovakia to be a full-time missionary. For nearly three years I traveled all over central Europe preaching the gospel. It is still one of the greatest seasons of my life.

I moved back to the States to go to seminary and had every intention of going back to the mission field. I remember coming back filled with passion and drive to see the nations come to Christ. It was literally like a fire burning inside of me.

And then, the strangest thing began to happen. Without even noticing it, as I got busy with school and settled back into a normal American life, the fire began to go out. I remember, after just a few months back home, realizing the fire was almost gone.

At that moment, God taught me a very important lesson about missions: every man must continue to fuel the fire for missions. Because we all tend to be self-centered and consumed with our little world, we have to fight to stay passionate about the lost.

This begins in our own passionate and daily pursuit of the presence of God. A man will never be passionate about spreading the presence of God unless he is passionate about experiencing the presence of God. Remember, the presence flows into Eden and then out of Eden. In the same way, God desires for His presence to flow into you and then out of you.

Where there is no passion flowing in, there will never be passion flowing out.

You can continue to fuel that fire by reading missionary biographies of men like Hudson Taylor, Adoniram Judson, Jim Elliot, and David Brainerd. You fuel the fire by spending time with those who are on mission with God and excited about it. You fuel the fire by praying regularly for unreached people groups.

> God desires for His presence to flow into you and then out of you.

But I think the most effective way to fuel the fire is by participating in short-term mission trips. Truthfully, I believe that for this book to be most effective, it will be discussed in men's groups, and then followed by a mission trip. There is nothing that takes the place of seeing the multitudes for yourself, and personally engaging in the mission of God. Find a church that is taking a short-term trip, and join them.

But we also fuel that fire by having lost people in our home, engaging people in conversations about the Lord, making friends with those who don't know Jesus, and sacrificially serving those less fortunate. The reality is—the more you engage in the mission, the more passion you begin to feel about the mission. But you must get started.

You need a mission. You need to be a part of something great. You need a cause to fight for. You need a compelling vision. Satan knows this, so his tactic is to get men to spend their life on a thousand frivolous things all done out of a desire to fill that void caused by the monotony of everyday life. But none of those lesser things will ever fulfill the longing for a mission.

The mission of God is the noblest, most adventurous and compelling cause in all of the world. It is what you have been created for. It is the great calling of your life. Every moment of every day is about being on a mission with God. And it begins now. It begins where you are. It begins with declaring and displaying the gospel to your neighbor. And it does not end until the last unreached people group hears the glorious message of Jesus Christ and people from every nation, tribe, and nation stand before the throne giving their worship to Jesus Christ (Rev. 7:9).

Discussion Questions

1. Even though men were created for a mission, why is it so challenging for men to engage in the mission of God?

2. What is the biggest thing that keeps you personally from engaging in God's mission on a regular basis?

3. How can you specifically make the mission of God more of a priority in your life?

4. What practical steps can you take right now to engage in the mission of God?

Chapter 9

ZEAL

THERE IS ONE moment in the life of Jesus that seems to surprise us more than any other.

A moment we don't immediately know how to process. It's a moment that does not seem to fit our image and expectations of Him. A moment that shows us something about Him we might not have seen before. It's a moment we don't expect.

When we read the Gospels, we expect His miracles. We expect His preaching, power, and authority. When we come to the end of the story, we expect His death, burial, and even His resurrection. We have been prepared for those moments.

What we don't expect is for Him to take the time to carefully handcraft a whip and use it to drive people out of the temple. We don't expect Him to pour out the coins of the money-changers, overturn tables, and declare, "Do not make my father's house a house of trade" (John 2:16). We don't expect Him to do it during the busiest time of the year when the temple was swarming with people, birds, and animals. And, we don't expect Him to do it twice.

The first time He does this is only recorded in John's Gospel (John 2:13–17), and it happened at the beginning of His ministry, right after His first miracle. The second time is recorded by Matthew, Mark, and Luke (Matt. 21:12–13; Mark 11:15–19; Luke 19:45), just days before His death. The first time He drove people out and the second time He blocked them from coming in.

Jesus only celebrated the Passovers four times during His public ministry. And at half of those, He ran through the temple, turning over tables, driving people out, yelling about His Father's house, and causing massive chaos. The last one seems to have been the final straw for the religious leaders of the day (Mark 11:18).

When you read these encounters, it almost feels as if something came over Him. It does not seem as if He went to the temple looking for a fight, but looking to worship. Instead, it feels like He was overcome by something. Something supernatural. And the reason it feels that way is because that is exactly what happened.

What came over Jesus in those moments can be summarized in one word: *zeal*.

John tells us that as the disciples tried to process this moment, they remembered what David said in Psalm 69:9: "Zeal for your house has consumed me." Through the revelation of the Holy Spirit, the disciples understood this psalm to be speaking of Jesus.

In those moments, as Jesus saw what was happening in the temple, Jesus was overcome with zeal. He was actually, as the psalmist said, "consumed" with zeal. And it is the same zeal that should consume us.

In Titus 2, after giving specific instruction to the people of the church, Paul says,

> For the grace of God has appeared, bringing salvation for all people, training us to renounce ungodliness and worldly passions, and to live self-controlled, upright, and godly lives in the present age, waiting for our blessed hope, the appearing of the glory of our great God and Savior Jesus Christ, who gave himself for us to redeem us from all lawlessness and to purify for himself a people for his own possession who are zealous for good works. (vv. 11–14)

God has always had a people. God has always been assembling a people for His own possession (Exod. 19:5; Ezek. 37:23). His plan has always been to choose, rescue, and redeem, and use a people to manifest His glory. And His intention has always been that these people, whom He has called by His name and chosen for His glory, would be zealous for good works.

The Titus Ten contains a lot of information. It is intended to be foundational. It is deeply rooted in truth and is meant to be a theological framework for your life. That is intentional. Not only because it is the truth that leads to godliness (Titus 1:2), but because one of the underlying goals of this book is to develop men who think biblically. The church desperately needs men who are saturated with the truth of God's Word.

> If there is one thing I hope this book will produce, it is zeal for godliness.

But, the real prayer in writing this book is that the truth would be the impetus to zeal. If there is one thing I hope this book will produce, it is zeal for godliness. Because what the church desperately needs from men, more than anything else, is zeal for God.

A Zeal for God

The dictionary defines *zeal* as "great energy or enthusiasm in pursuit of a cause or an objective."[15] It can also be defined as an "eagerness and ardent interest in the pursuit of something" or an "intense emotion compelling action."[16] It is synonymous with words like *passion*, *enthusiasm*, and *fervor*.

Yet, as the definitions show, it is more than just a feeling. It is an overwhelming enthusiasm that leads to action. Like the overwhelming enthusiasm that led Jesus to cleanse the temple.

The kind of zeal that we need is a zeal for God. This kind of zeal is defined for us in two passages in the book of Romans.

In Romans 10, Paul is talking about his deep love for the Jews and longing for them to be saved. He describes them by saying, "They have a zeal for God, but not according to knowledge" (Rom. 10:2). Zeal is not only what led Jesus to confront the religious leaders of the day and drive them out of the temple; zeal is also what led those same religious leaders not to rest until they ensured Jesus would die. It is possible to have a zeal for God and go to hell.

Zeal for God is rooted in the knowledge of God (Rom. 10:2). Knowledge of God does not water down our zeal. Good theology does not fill the head while killing the heart; it is the impetus for godly zeal. The times in my life I have been the most zealous for God are the times in which I have been almost overwhelmed by the reality of God. A zeal that does not accord with knowledge is dangerous and destructive.

> Good theology does not fill the head while killing the heart; it is the impetus for godly zeal.

183

Godly zeal is not only rooted in knowledge; it is boiling with passion. In Romans 12:11 Paul says, "Do not be slothful in zeal, be fervent in spirit." The opposite of being slothful in zeal is being fervent in spirit. The word *fervent* means "boiling." It means burning passion and intensity. Zeal has strong feelings, emotions, and intensity. Zeal affects your spirit. Zeal consumes your emotions. Zeal takes over.

Jesus could have walked into the temple and preached a sermon titled "Den of Thieves." But instead, He ran through the temple overcome with burning emotions. He was angry. He was jealous. He was hurt. He was grieved. He was boiling with passion and intensity. He was consumed with zeal.

Zeal is rooted in knowledge and boiling with passion. But that is not all. Zeal is also manifested in action. Every definition of *zeal* says that it is a feeling of intensity that leads to action. And that is exactly what we see in the last part of Romans 12:11: "Do not be slothful in zeal, be fervent in spirit, serve the Lord." As Titus 2:14 says, God saved us that we might be "zealous for good works." Zeal is not just a feeling. Zeal is an action. Zeal serves. Zeal moves. Zeal is unable to stand still.

Paul concludes this little letter to Titus with two strong admonitions. He says, "I want you to insist on these things, so that those who have believed in God may be careful to devote themselves to good works" (3:8). And again, he says, "And let our people learn to devote themselves to good works, so as to help cases of urgent need, and not be unfruitful" (3:14). Instead of being like the rebellious men who were "detestable, disobedient, and unfit for any good works" (1:16), God is calling us to be men devoted to good works. Men who are actively seeking to know Christ and make Him known. Men of zeal.

Knowledge, passion, and action. If you remove any of these, you no longer have godly zeal. There is no zeal without knowledge. I get so tired of people acting as if somehow theology leads to dryness. The source of all Christian zeal is a right understanding of the glory, holiness, perfection, sovereignty, and all-out magnificence of God! Those who have a small vision of God will have no zeal. Zeal begins when one starts to see God in all of His glory!

There is also no zeal without the white-hot, all-consuming, passion of the soul. Godly zeal makes your soul boil. In the same way that a teapot cannot help but whistle when the water begins to boil, your soul cannot help but be filled with passion when you begin to experience the zeal of the Lord.

Think about the working together of knowledge, passion, and action as Jesus cleansed the temple. And think about how many men you know who have one, or even two of those, but not all three. Think about the men who love truth, but have no

> A head full of knowledge, a heart full of passion, and a life full of action— that is godly zeal.

boiling passion. Or the men who love truth but not action. Think about the men who have boiling passion about something, but it is not rooted in truth. Or think about the men who love to act, but it is void of truth and passion for God. If you remove any one of these three, you do not have godly zeal.

A head full of knowledge, a heart full of passion, and a life full of action—that is godly zeal. And that is what God has saved you for. Nothing less.

Ablaze with Glory

God does not just want a people; He wants a zealous people. He always has. This is what it means to love the Lord your God with all your heart, soul, and strength (Deut. 6:5). His intention has always been that our hearts be filled with passion and affection for Him.

Zeal is not just another character quality we cultivate; zeal is a primary mark of the people of God. God demands it. He hates anything other than it. And we should not settle for anything less than it.

When Andrea and I were engaged, her father asked me to take a road trip with him. On that trip, he asked what my favorite book of the Bible was. I don't remember what I said, but I remember what he said. When I asked him the same question, he said, "My favorite book of the Bible, without question, is the book of Revelation." I was surprised by his response. I quickly responded, "Really? I've never liked the book of Revelation." To which he responded, "Well, you would only like the book of Revelation if you liked the glory of Jesus Christ." *Ouch.*

He was right. Among all the seals, scrolls, and trumpets, I had missed the most important part of the entire revelation: the glory of Jesus. It is a glory that we see in Revelation 1, as John describes the Son of Man.

> Then I turned to see the voice that was speaking to me, and on turning I saw seven golden lampstands, and in the midst of the lampstands one like a son of man, clothed with a long robe and with a golden sash around his chest. The hairs of his head were white, like white wool, like snow. His eyes were like a flame of fire, his feet were like burnished bronze, refined in a furnace, and his voice was like the roar of many waters. In his right hand he held seven stars, from his mouth came a sharp two-edged sword, and his face was like the sun shining in full strength. (Rev. 1:12–16)

This is a vision of Jesus Christ in blazing splendor. We see Jesus, ablaze with glory. Everything about Him, from His robe to His face, is on fire. When you read this description, you are not only gripped by the words themselves, but by the weight of the words. The weight of glory. The blinding blaze of glory.

Surrounding Jesus, ablaze with glory, are seven lampstands, symbolizing seven churches. And these churches are intended to be the bearers of that blaze. They are, in a sense, the holders of the fire. The church is to be the place in which the blazing glory of God is experienced and displayed.

That helps us make sense of God's absolute disgust with the church in Laodicea, which was not ablaze with anything (Rev. 3:14-21). This church was neither cold nor hot. This church was lukewarm. It was useless and disgusting. It had no passion, intensity, fervency, or enthusiasm.

But those church members didn't see themselves this way. "For you say, I am rich, I have prospered, and I need nothing, not realizing that you are wretched, pitiable, poor, blind, and naked" (Rev. 3:17). They didn't even notice they were void of the one thing they were intended to have—fire! They existed to be the holders of the blazing-hot glory of Jesus but instead were satisfied with being disgustingly tepid.

John Stott was right when he said,

> Perhaps none of the seven letters is more appropriate to the church at the beginning of the twenty-first century than this. It describes vividly the respectable, nominal, rather sentimental, skin-deep religiosity which is so widespread among us today. Our

> Christianity is flabby and anemic. We appear
> to have taken a lukewarm bath of religion.[17]

So many men are like the church in Laodicea. And the saddest part is not that they are lukewarm, but that they don't even notice. The normal Christian experience for most men is one of lukewarm religion instead of white-hot passion. And Jesus hates it!

Why? Because Jesus, who is ablaze with Glory, created you to be filled with His glory and make His glory known to the nations. The way He intends to do that is by filling you with boiling zeal for Him. The call of Jesus on your life is nothing less than to be set ablaze with zeal as He is ablaze with glory!

The normal Christian experience for most men is one of lukewarm religion instead of white-hot passion.

Repent

The solution for our lukewarm heart is the same as the solution for the lukewarm church: "be zealous and repent" (Rev. 3:19). *Repent.* Why? Because it is a sin to be lukewarm.

Let me say that again: It is a sin to be lukewarm.

Being lukewarm takes that which is most glorious and makes it appear mundane. Our lukewarm hearts cannot make His glory known.

It is amazing to think that what seems to be the normal experience of most men is a sin against God. Most men live with no passion, affection, desire, or longing for God. But being passionless about God is a sin.

If there is no zeal in your life, you must repent. Acknowledge your lack of passion for God, see it as a sin, ask Him to forgive you for that sin, and then turn from that sin. Repentance is a conscious act to turn from our sin to God. And we need God's help to do this.

When I was a senior in high school, I was the epitome of lukewarm. In my mind, I wanted to long for God, but I had no actual longing for Him. I am not even sure how to explain it. I wanted to want God. I hated my mediocrity. I didn't want it anymore. I knew it was not only disgusting to God; it was disgusting to me. It made life miserable. I knew that God had more, and I wanted it.

So, I did the only thing I knew to do. I got on my knees every day and asked God to give me a desire for Him. My daily prayer was that simple: "Lord, I want to want you." I prayed it over and over again. And as I prayed, God began to answer. My desire for God grew. And as my desire for God grew, my pursuit of God increased. And as my pursuit of God increased, my zeal for God increased.

This is how God begins to cultivate zeal in us. It begins with a hatred for the lukewarm life we are so accustomed to. Our passionless and lifeless relationship with Jesus must disgust us as much as it disgusts God. We must see it as sin and turn from it. And then, we must turn to God and ask Him to give us the zeal that comes from Him. This is repentance.

I am confident that, as you see your lack of zeal, acknowledge it to God, and tell Him you want more, He will answer that prayer. God is the rewarder of those who seek Him (Heb. 11:6). He wants you to be zealous.

Do not resist the desire in your heart for zeal. Even if it is just a glimmer of desire. Pursue it. Start now. Get on your knees, acknowledge your lack of passion, confess it, turn from it, ask God to change it, and then begin turning toward Him in obedience.

Pursuing Zeal

After the call to repentance, in the most matter-of-fact way possible, we are told to "be zealous." This is a direct command. Be zealous. Stop being lukewarm. Stop settling for a life that has no passion for God. This is not only God's intention for you; it is His expectation.

The command to "be zealous" is more helpful than you might imagine. It is helpful because it tells us that zeal is not something we just passively hope for; it is something we aggressively pursue. In the same way our Christian life generally is both wholly dependent on the work of God in us and cultivated by the constant effort of our Spirit-infused will, so zeal is a work God must do and a work we must pursue.

A. W. Tozer said, "We have as much of God as we actually want."[18] He's exactly right. We don't have zeal because we have not pursued zeal. God wants to give us more of Himself. He wants to give us a fresh and life-changing vision of His glory that fills us with a blazing passion for Him. And He wants us to pursue it.

Romans 12:11 tells us the same thing: "Do not be slothful in zeal, be fervent in spirit." Slothful means lazy or sluggish. It is possible to be slothful in zeal, meaning we have become lazy in our pursuit of it. We don't have zeal because we have not pursued it. We have not pursued it because we have settled for less. God wants to change that.

Although there are many ways we can cultivate zeal in our lives, there are two essentials: the Word and the Spirit. To have zeal, we must have a mind filled with the knowledge of God and a spirit continually being set on fire by His Spirit.

If truth is the foundation of zeal, then the Word is essential to zeal. Your zeal will grow as your knowledge of God grows. This is the paradigm of Revelation 1–3. What we need first, before anything else, is a fresh and consuming vision of Jesus Christ. We need to see Jesus in His blazing glory for our hearts to be filled with blazing zeal. We need to see Jesus as He is revealed in God's Word.

We need to feel the weight of His glory like John did in Revelation 1. Our zeal increases as we dig into the deeper things of God. As we go beyond the casual reading of Scripture into the careful study of Scripture. As we read books of the Bible over and over and over again. As we seek to understand the true meaning and intention behind passages. A casual reading of Scripture will not get us very far in our pursuit of zeal. Zealous people know God. They pursue God. They have come to see more of His glory in the pages of Scripture.

> We need to see Jesus in His blazing glory for our hearts to be filled with blazing zeal.

But zeal is not only a matter of the mind; it is a matter of the spirit. "Do not be slothful in zeal, be fervent in spirit" (Rom. 12:11). For your spirit to be filled with the same zeal Jesus manifested in the temple, you must be filled with the same Spirit that filled Jesus. The only hope we have of being zealous for God is by the Spirit of God lighting our spirits on fire with His presence.

In the same way, we are told to "be zealous," we are told to "be filled with the Spirit" (Eph. 5:18). For years I felt like being filled with the Spirit was something that had to be done *to me*. I would just pray, "Lord, fill me with Your Spirit" and just wait and hope He did it. But the apostle Paul tells us otherwise.

In Ephesians 5:18, Paul gives us an illustration to teach us how to be filled with the Spirit. "Do not get drunk with wine, . . . but be filled with the Spirit." Meaning, a person is filled with the Spirit in the same way a person gets drunk with wine—by drinking a lot.

Jesus said, "If anyone thirsts, let him come to me and drink. Whoever believes in me, as the Scripture has said, 'Out of his heart will flow rivers of living water.' Now this he said about the Spirit" (John 7:37–39). We aren't passively filled with the Spirit, and we aren't passively filled with zeal. The more we go after God, the more God's Spirit puts a fire of zeal in our spirit.

There is such simplicity in this. Your zeal will be in direct proportion to your pursuit of God.

You must not only fight *for* zeal, you must also fight *against* that which kills zeal. First Thessalonians 5:19 says, "Do not quench the Spirit." Another way to say this is, "Do not put out the Spirit's fire." The Spirit of God lights a fire of zeal in our spirits for God, but sin puts out the fire. Holiness puts fuel on the fire; sin puts water on the fire.

When we think about the consequences of sin, we most often think about the potential long-term consequences on our own lives, our families, our churches, or even our careers. But we don't think about the daily consequences of putting out the fire of godly zeal.

One of our primary motives in fighting sin should be our desire to be zealous for God. We want our lives to be filled with godly, Christ-exalting, red-hot, boiling zeal for God. The zeal that moves from the head to the heart to the hands. And that longing should keep us from sin.

Zeal begins with an all-consuming vision of the glory of Jesus Christ. Zeal then moves to a burning-hot passion and affection for Jesus. And finally, zeal manifests itself in good works for the name of Jesus. It is not godly zeal unless it moves from our head to our heart, to our hands.

There are many other practical ways to continue to cultivate zeal. We need to spend time with people who have a zeal for God, listen to preachers who are zealous for God, read missionary biographies, read books about the character and nature of God, and listen to worship music that raises our affections for God.

The key is this: You must actively pursue things that fuel the fire of zeal for God and actively kill those things that put the fire out. Because the temperature of your heart will affect the temperature of those around you.

> You must actively pursue things that fuel the fire of zeal for God and actively kill those things that put the fire out.

Men, You Set the Temperature

When Andrea was diagnosed with cancer, God taught me a defining principle of godly manhood: men set the temperature. When our entire family was battling the reality of Andrea's sickness, I realized very quickly that the spiritual, emotional, and moral temperature of my home was determined by the temperature of my own heart. I can't explain all the reasons this is true, but I know it's true. I see it played out every day.

The temperature of my heart when I walk in the door from work, in many ways, will determine the temperature of my home the rest of the night. The temperature of our staff will be determined by the temperature of my heart when I walk into a meeting. The temperature of our Sunday services will be determined by the temperature of my heart when I stand up to preach.

In some supernatural and unexplainable way, God has so ordained it that the men set the temperature. Men can raise the heat or chill the air. And this is not determined by our intentions, hopes, or desires. This is determined by the temperature of our hearts.

The first battle we fight, every day, is the battle for godly zeal. It is the battle to begin each day by fueling the fire through time in God's Word and pursuit of God's Spirit. It continues throughout the day as you aggressively fight any sin or distraction that might diminish the fire. The fire of godly zeal must be your great pursuit.

Where Are the Zealous Men?

Tears are welling up in my eyes as I write these words. I think about the perfect zeal that Jesus displayed in the temple. I think about the depth of His passion and the cost of His actions. I think about Him being overcome with white-hot affection for His Father and His Father's house. I think of Him seeing what was happening in the temple and then making His whip and bringing it back to the temple. I think about the holiness, power, and example of His zeal.

Then I think about the love of God the Father displayed in the sacrifice of His only Son. I think about the desire of God the Father to redeem a people for Himself who would possess the same kind of zeal as His Son. I think about Jesus, captured, beaten, and publicly shamed to bring us to glory. I think about the cost of saving us and making us into a zealous people.

And then, I think about the men I see on Sunday morning. They are holding a cup of coffee while the congregation is singing of the glories of Christ. They do not join with the great choir of the redeemed and open their mouths in praise to God. I see their hands in their pockets instead of being lifted high in praise to Jesus. I think about the look on their faces when the truth of God's Word is being declared. I think about the glazed look in their eyes when we stand before them and plead for someone to take the gospel to the nations. And I just can't help but wonder, *Where is the zeal for God?*

- Why aren't the men singing the loudest?
- Why aren't their hands raised the highest?
- Why are they not listening most intently?
- Why are they not the first to serve, the first to stand, the first to kneel, the first to respond to every word of God?

Men, there is too much at stake in these times for us to settle for anything less than godly zeal. The current of our culture is too strong. The headwinds against the mission are too great. The darkness of the world is too overwhelming. The attacks of the enemy are too strong. We need men filled with godly zeal.

> Men, there is too much at stake in these times for us to settle for anything less than godly zeal.

Make godly zeal the great pursuit of your life. Do all you can to make sure your heart burns hot with a consuming passion for the glory of King Jesus. The kind of passion that not only lights a fire in your heart, but in the

hearts of everyone around you. May the Lord raise up a generation of men, like Jesus, consumed with zeal. God help us.

Discussion Questions

1. The word *zeal* can be misunderstood. Just to be clear, state
the three parts of zeal given in this chapter.

2. Why does it matter so much that you be a person of godly
zeal? Why do we need zealous men? What would be the result
if we had them or did not have them?

3. Would your life be more characterized by lukewarm religion
or white-hot passion?

4. What practical specific steps can you take to cultivate zeal?
What needs to be added or removed in order to do this?

5. How can you better set the temperature in your home,
workplace, or other relationships?

Chapter 10

INVESTMENTS

THE BOOK OF Acts is filled with stories of solid men. But my favorite of them all is Barnabas.

Barnabas was a strong man with a good reputation. His name was actually "Joseph," but the apostles called him "Barnabas," a name that means "son of encouragement" (Acts 4:36). When you read the stories of how God used him, you'll understand why they changed his name.

When the apostles found out that the church in Antioch was growing rapidly, they needed to send someone to encourage them. They sent Barnabas.

> The report of this came to the ears of the church in Jerusalem, and they sent Barnabas to Antioch. When he came and saw the grace of God, he was glad, and he exhorted them all to remain faithful to the Lord with

steadfast purpose, for he was a good man, full of the Holy Spirit and of faith. And a great many people were added to the Lord. (Acts 11:22–24)

This perfectly summarizes the ministry of Barnabas. His primary message was to "remain faithful." Barnabas was always speaking blessing and life into the members of the early church who were tempted to give up, and he was the apostle's go-to man when a church needed spiritual encouragement.

Barnabas spent his life investing in believers. One of his greatest investments was in the life of a newly converted Jewish leader by the name of Saul. Saul was there when Stephen was martyred, and he approved of the killing (Acts 8:1). He then spent his time doing door-to-door un-evangelism. Acts 8:3 says, "But Saul was ravaging the church, and entering house after house, he dragged off men and women and committed them to prison." Paul went to the high priest and asked permission to go to Damascus and arrest every Christian he could find (9:1–2). He was an evil man who despised Christians. But on his way to Damascus to forcibly imprison Christians, he met Jesus and was radically saved (9:4–19). We know Saul as Paul, which is the name he used more commonly after his conversion.[19]

Paul immediately began to meet with the disciples and preach. But there was a problem. He had made a bit of a name for himself as the guy who killed and imprisoned Christians.

So when he tried to join the Christians in Jerusalem, they were a little nervous and weren't so sure what to do with him.

> And when he had come to Jerusalem, he attempted to join the disciples. And they were all afraid of him, for they did not believe that he was a disciple. But Barnabas took him and brought him to the apostles and declared to them how on the road he had seen the Lord, who spoke to him, and how at Damascus he had preached boldly in the name of Jesus. . . . And when the brothers learned this, they brought him down to Caesarea and sent him off to Tarsus. (Acts 9:26–30)

Two words changed the situation: "But Barnabas." Everyone was terrified of Paul. And understandably so. They didn't want to let him in the church. What if it was all a ploy?

"But Barnabas." It was Barnabas who first believed in Paul, invested in him, encouraged him, and brought him into the church. Without Barnabas speaking on his behalf, there is no indication that the church would have ever believed Paul. But Barnabas was doing what he always did—investing in men.

From that moment on, a beautiful friendship emerged between Paul and Barnabas. Their giftings and passions were a perfect fit, and together they planted and encouraged many churches. And it all started with Barnabas's decision to make a risky investment.

At the beginning of his Christian life, Paul learned from Barnabas the power of investing in others. From those early days until his last days, investing in others was in Paul's spiritual DNA. It was the kind of investment he received from Barnabas that would lead Paul to make that kind of investment in countless others. And, to teach that this kind of investing is what every man is called to do.

In Paul's last letter, he told Timothy, "You then, my child, be strengthened by the grace that is in Christ Jesus, and what you have heard from me in the presence of many witnesses entrust to faithful men, who will be able to teach others also" (2 Tim. 2:1–2). Barnabas invested heavily in Paul. Paul invested heavily in Timothy. And now Timothy was instructed to take that investment and invest it in others. This is how God builds men: investments.

Men Are the Method

In his classic book on discipleship, Robert Coleman said:

> It all started by Jesus calling a few men to follow Him. This revealed immediately the direction his evangelistic strategy would take. His concern was not with programs to teach the multitudes, but with men whom the

multitudes would follow. Remarkable as it may seem, Jesus started to gather these men before he ever organized an evangelistic campaign or even preached a sermon in public. Men were to be his method of winning the world to God.[20]

"Men were to be his method." You can spend as much time as you want on the methods of Jesus, but in the end, you will discover His primary method was people. Jesus invested in men who would then lead other men, who would go on to lead families, churches, and communities for the glory of God. People are the mission, and people are the method.

> Jesus invested in men who would then lead other men, who would go on to lead families, churches, and communities for the glory of God.

Paul learned this from Jesus. He experienced it from Barnabas and taught it to everyone he invested in. Including Titus.

Teach and Model

After identifying godly men, putting them into leadership, and teaching them how to lead the church, Paul tells

Titus what else he must do. "But as for you, teach what accords with sound doctrine" (Titus 2:1). Then, Paul gets specific. He tells Titus to give specific instruction to the older men, older women, younger women, younger men, and the "bondservants" in the church.

Paul knew that for the church to thrive, each one of these groups needed to know how to live. And Paul knew they would get this clarity from both right doctrine and right living, or application of that doctrine. Paul even ends this practical instruction in Titus 2 by telling Titus to "declare these things; exhort, and rebuke with all authority. Let no one disregard you" (Titus 2:15). These people needed the kind of sound doctrine that leads to a solid life.

But Titus was not only to "teach" these things; he was to "model these things." Paul says, "Show yourself in all respects to be a model of good works, and in your teaching show integrity, dignity, and sound speech that cannot be condemned, so that an opponent may be put to shame, having nothing evil to say about us" (Titus 2:7–8).

This word *model* means "a prototype or a pattern" (see 1 Cor. 10:6; Phil. 3:17; 1 Thess. 1:7). What the church needed was not only a good teacher; they needed a good model. They had never seen a "prototype" of a godly man. These were first-generation Christians. None of these men grew up in Christian homes. None of them had fathers who had taken seriously the call of Deuteronomy 6 and Ephesians 5:4 to raise their children in the things of the Lord. And that is why when Paul stopped in Crete and saw this dysfunctional church, he did not just leave them a letter; he left them a person. He left Titus there at the church to model for them what it looks like to be a man of God. They needed to hear the truth declared, and they needed to see the truth worked out in real life.

Every man needs to hear sound teaching and see good examples. Every man needs a prototype of godliness. Many passages of Scripture show us a father is to fulfill that role for his son (Deut. 6; 1 Thess. 2:11; Ps. 128; 1 Tim. 3:2–5). But, as strange as it might seem, men need more than that. Men also need a church.

> Every man needs to hear sound teaching and see good examples.

Even men who were raised in a great home with a godly father need the investment of other men. A godly father who knows the Word of God would agree that his son needs the support of other men in the church. My children not only need my continual investment; they desperately need others to come alongside me and invest. The local church has always been the place where God intended for those relationships to be cultivated.

But the vast majority of men did not have a father that made that kind of investment. We have a generation of men who are longing for someone to invest in them. We have a generation of men who have never seen a good prototype of godliness. And God's solution for this situation has always been the church. It is in the context of a local church where men who have never heard manhood taught or modeled find someone to show them.

Older Men and Younger Men

In order for the church to fulfill its God-given role of investing in men, it needs both older men and younger men. A few years ago, I had a Sunday off, and I went to visit a prominent, rapidly growing church with a well-known pastor. I was deeply blessed and encouraged to experience for myself just how the Lord was moving in this local congregation. But after being there for a few minutes, as I looked around, I noticed there weren't any older people. I saw a few bald heads, but no gray heads. This was a large church with no presence of the older generation. That's a problem.

When I first began teaching the book of Titus to men, I did so in groups of ten. One of my commitments was that each of these groups would have generational diversity. I would try to have two guys in their twenties, two in their thirties, two in their forties, and the rest would be fifty or older. I not only did this because it seems to be the model of the early church, but because this is one of the greatest joys of being in a local church. What a privilege to be in a place filled with men who need investment and men who can invest!

Because both older men and younger men are critical to spiritual growth, Titus 2 instructs both groups. The instruction to older men is not just good for older men; it is good for younger men. It gives a prototype—a model.

To an older man, Paul says, "be sober-minded, dignified, self-controlled, sound in faith, in love, and in steadfastness" (Titus 2:2). The first thing Paul says is that they should be "sober-minded." This means they should avoid extravagances and overindulgences. An older man should, because of his age and experience, be able to discern the things of greater importance and value. His priorities should be in the right order.

He should also be "dignified." This means he should be distinguished, serious-minded, and have qualities others respect. This man is not frivolous, trivial, or superficial. There is a marked maturity. This is in contrast to some older men who get older but remain immature. These words together indicate there should be sobriety and seriousness to older men that are not characteristic of younger men. They are to be able to demonstrate a sense of inner restraint and self-control.

An older man is also to be self-controlled. This means he should have discernment, discretion, and good judgment that come from walking with God. He should be able to control his passions and desires and reject foolish and worldly desires.

Finally, an older man should be sound in faith, love, and steadfastness. This is an incredible statement. To be sound means to be healthy, proper, and whole. It means to be solid as a rock. And an older man who loves Jesus should be solid as a rock in his faith, his love, and his steadfastness.

A man who is solid in his faith is well-grounded, wise, and does not waver. A man who is solid in his love has learned that love is not just a feeling; it is a decision. A man who is solid in his steadfastness knows how to endure hardship, to accept disappointments and failures. These men are not easily thrown off by trials and difficulties in their life or relationships. They are sound.

One of the most important truths we learn from this passage is that the greatest disgrace for an older man is to act like a younger man. If an older man wants to be relevant to a younger generation, he does not need to do so by trying to look and act like them. That just makes him look foolish. An older man becomes relevant to younger men by becoming the kind of older man described in Titus 2:2. Younger men don't need older men to be a cheap imitation of themselves; they need older men to be prototypes of a godly man.

Paul's instruction to younger men reveals just how much this is true. After a long list of qualities for an older man to cultivate, he only gives one thing to younger men: "Likewise, urge the younger men to be self-controlled" (v. 6).

That's it. One word for younger men—*self-control*. If a young man can learn how to make his own body his slave and submit himself to the authority of the Lord Jesus Christ, he will be on his way to becoming the kind of man God wants him to be. If he does not learn to be self-controlled, he will never be sober-minded, dignified, and sound.

> Younger men don't need older men to be a cheap imitation of themselves; they need older men to be prototypes of a godly man.

There are very few contexts in our culture in which older men and younger men are cultivating relationships. But if you only spend time with people your age, you are missing out on the kind of investment God has created you for.

Many older men are tempted to attend a church filled with older people. Younger men are tempted to attend a church with younger people. But I want to plead with you to resist that temptation. God's plan for the church is to be a place where multi-generational investments are made.

Find an Investor

For start-up companies to succeed, they almost always need investors. An investor is someone who believes in the company and will invest financial capital for the company to grow and expand. A more engaged investor might even invest his business expertise to help the company make good decisions. Companies need investors to succeed. So do you.

You need people who believe in you, see potential in you, and want to invest in your future. To become the man God wants you to become, you need godly men to invest in you. Sometimes this is a more formal, long-term investment, and sometimes it's an informal, short-term investment. Most likely, you will need some of both.

I always thought if I wrote a book like this, I would dedicate it to the men who invested in me over the years. But every time I started making a list, God kept bringing new people to my mind. I knew if I tried, I would forget people. As I look over the list, I realize that many of these men very intentionally invested in me. Men like Mike Griffin, Rob Kalpak, Barry St. Clair, Jim O'Neill, Danny Jones, Bill Elliff, Fred Hartley, and Steve Gaines took the time to speak into my life.

I also notice from the list that many of these men had no idea they invested in me. Through the years there have been countless other men whom I've asked to lunch, gone to for counsel, and sought out in difficult situations who all made life-changing investments into my life. I am a product of all those investments. Big ones and small ones.

When I came to pastor Prince Avenue in 2018, I was following a man named Bill Ricketts who had pastored this church for forty-three years. Pastors are often hesitant to go to a church where they have to follow a long-term leader. Especially when—like my case—the man was going to remain a member of the church. But instead of this being any type of hindrance to my ministry, it has become one of the greatest blessings of my ministry. Brother Bill and I meet once a month for lunch, and I have gone to him for counsel countless times. I have never asked him to mentor me. We don't have anything official. There is no agenda. There is no curriculum. We just meet for lunch. And with every lunch, he is investing in me. It has become one of the great joys of my life and ministry.

Proverbs 18:1 says, "Whoever isolates himself seeks his own desire; he breaks out against all sound judgment." Most men tend toward isolation. Even if it's not social isolation, it's spiritual isolation. For this reason, we must heed the warning and wisdom of Solomon and actively seek out men to invest in us. Isolation kills manhood.

Don't wait for a man to invite you into that process. You must take the initiative. And don't overthink it or overcomplicate it. You don't need a man to commit to meet with you every week for the next three years. Start by asking a man you respect for breakfast or lunch. Ask questions. Be honest. Seek his wisdom. And in doing so, you will not only honor the other man; you will benefit greatly.

Make an Investment

As you spend time with the Lord, grow in your faith, and pursue others to make investments in you, God will invest things in your heart that He intends for you to invest in others. Isn't this the way 2 Timothy 2:2 works? What has been invested in you, you invest in others.

Every year in our church we have a hard time finding men who will lead new discipleship groups. Many men will agree to be in one, but they don't want to lead one. Many of them would rather be a member of a group for five years than branch out and lead their group. I don't think this is primarily because of their fear of leading or unwillingness to take responsibility. I think it has a lot to do with their belief that they just don't have much to offer. But every man has had something invested in him; therefore, every man has something to invest.

When it comes to making investments in the lives of others, we tend to over-complicate it. And when we over-complicate it, we feel inadequate. You must fight that feeling of inadequacy by reminding yourself of this simple truth: God has invested much in you. Your responsibility is simply to take what God has invested in you and invest it into the lives of others.

Part of this investment is biblical truth and spiritual disciplines. When God teaches us new truths from His Word, those need to be invested. When God teaches you how to gain victory over sin and temptation, that is something to invest in others. Any biblical truth or practical application of that truth is something that has been invested in you. And all of those are to be invested in others.

Just a few months ago I reached out to an older man on our staff and asked him to help me learn how to have a more effective prayer life. I knew he had a vibrant prayer life, and I wanted to learn. In a two-hour lunch, he made a great investment in my life. And it was simple things he had learned over the years about how to be more focused and effective in prayer.

But we must think of our ability to invest in others as more than just the investment of biblical truths. Every experience in your life is part of what has been invested in you. Although the primary means by which God teaches us truth is His Word, He also teaches us through others, through experiences, and through suffering.

I distinctly remember in one of my early morning Titus Ten groups when a young man opened up about some significant problems he was having in his marriage. We were all shocked. We had no idea these struggles were going on. And it was complicated. A lot of this was caused by some recent pressures at work that led to him being irritable and angry. Those pressures were caused by some previous failures at work that fed his insecurities and worry that he might lose his job. He also had some unresolved hurt in the past that was starting to come to light. All of this made him withdraw from his family and become passive and angry. His marriage was a wreck. And for the first time in his life, he was opening up about it.

Everyone listened as he wept and poured out his heart. What he didn't know is that a few years before this, an older man named Jim had taken me to lunch and told me his life story. Jim's story was almost identical. And by God's providence, Jim was in this group.

I didn't say anything about it. We listened to this young man and prayed for him. And then, after the group was over, I watched Jim go to this young man, put his arm around him, and talk to him. That was the beginning of a friendship that lasted for many years—and a friendship that ended up helping save this young man's marriage. What was Jim doing? He was investing what he learned from his experience in the life of another person.

When my wife was thirty-four, she was diagnosed with stage-4 cancer. Word spread quickly about her sickness and people from all over the world began to pray for her during that time. By God's grace, she is now cancer-free. A few months ago, years after my wife's cancer, I received an e-mail from a pastor who is an acquaintance of mine. He told me about a young woman in his church who had just been diagnosed with cancer. The husband was struggling, and his pastor remembered we had been through the same thing. He asked me to contact the young man and talk with him. I texted him this morning. I don't have a lot of answers, but I can invest in him what was invested in me during some of the most brutal days of my life.

You have something to invest. I know that for a fact. I know it because there is no man on this planet in whom God has not invested. If no other man has ever invested in you, God has invested in you. Everything from your background, to your family, to your work, to your greatest highs and your deepest lows, are investments that God has made in you. And those are the things God wants you to invest in others.

You have something to invest.

These types of investments can take many different forms. Things like gathering men for weekly prayer and Bible study, doing a Bible study with a new believer, or even taking some men through this book are great ways to invest. But so are simple things like praying for someone, speaking a word of encouragement, asking someone how they are doing, writing someone a note, and helping someone financially.

The irony of investing in others is that it is always an investment in yourself. Some of the greatest growth in your life will come from the investments you make in the life of others. I have found the more I resist my tendency to be isolated and choose to invest in others, the more the Lord invests in me.

A Humbling Reminder

No generation in the Old Testament experienced more of God's supernatural power and blessing than Joshua's generation. This is the generation that finally possessed the promised land and experienced the fullness of all the promises God had made to their ancestors. The book of Joshua is filled with so many victories and miracles and blessings. No generation had more invested in them than Joshua's generation.

But Judges 2:10 says, when talking about the Joshua generation, "And all that generation also were gathered to their fathers. And there arose another generation after them who did not know the Lord or the work that he had done for Israel." The rest of the book of Judges is a humbling reminder of how quickly the next generation can lose all the blessings their fathers experienced. The rest of the Old Testament reveals the consequences.

What happened? How could everything be lost so quickly? The answer seems to be that Joshua's generation, while having so much invested in them and enjoying so much of the fruit of that investment, failed to pass it on to the next generation.

So much has been invested in you. This means you have so much to invest. More than you could ever imagine. Don't let the enemy tell you anything different. God wants to use you to make an investment that will long outlive your own life.

If We Turn to the Right . . .

In 1888, Charles Spurgeon said,

> It is today as it was in the Reformers' days.
> Decision is needed. Here is the day for the
> man, where is the man for the day? We who
> have had the gospel passed to us by martyrs'
> hands dare not trifle with it, nor sit by and
> hear it denied by traitors, who pretend to love
> it, but inwardly abhor every word of it. . . .
> Look you, sires, there are ages yet to come. If
> the Lord does not speedily appear, there will
> come another generation, and another, and all
> these generations will be tainted and injured
> if we are not faithful to God and His truth
> today. We have come to a turning-point in the
> road. If we turn to the right, mayhap our chil-
> dren and our children's children will go that
> way; but if we turn to the left, generations yet
> unborn will curse our names for having been
> unfaithful to God and to His word.[21]

Today is the day for the man; where is the man for the
day? The answer is, you are the man for the day. In your context, in your church, in your workplace, in your family—you
are the man for the day. You are a part of that next generation
of faithful men that not only influence their generation, but

the generation to come. Your life matters more than you can ever imagine. Not just for this generation, but for the next one.

Every chapter of this book has challenged individual men to become the man God has called them to become. It has been a call to action. A call to be a faithful doer. But, if along the way we do not become faithful investors, we will fail to leave the church with a new generation of men they so desperately need. Our responsibility is not to just our generation, but to the generation that comes after us.

May God help us to become the men God has called us to become and intentionally raise up another generation of men to do the same.

Discussion Questions

1. Have you ever had someone like a "Barnabas" in your life? How did that person invest in your life and what affect did that have on you?

2. Do you currently have anyone investing in you in a formal or nonformal way? Can you think of a specific person you would like to learn from or spend some time with? How could you initiate that?

3. Thinking about 2 Timothy 2:2, what personal experiences, knowledge, or skills do you believe God has entrusted to you that could be entrusted to others?

4. Is there anyone in your life who you feel you should invest in? What steps do you need to take to do that?

5. In what specific ways can you take what has been invested in you from *The Titus Ten* and invest it in someone else?

One Final Word

DIRECTION

I DON'T REMEMBER a time in which I wasn't generally discouraged with my spiritual progress. I've always felt like I should be further down the road than I am. If you had asked me twenty years ago how far I would be down the pathway toward mature manhood at this point, I assure you I would have said I'd be a lot farther down the pathway. Sometimes I think, *Josh, you are forty-seven years old! How in the world are you still struggling this way?!*

But a few years ago, the Lord deeply encouraged me by a fresh understanding of following Jesus. For most of my life, my walk with Jesus was all about distance. I evaluated everything by how far I had gone, how much progress I had made, and how much I had accomplished. For me, what mattered most, was distance.

There is certainly something good and holy about wanting to make progress. Jesus expects us to be making progress.

At times, Jesus genuinely seems frustrated with His disciples by their lack of progress (Mark 8:21; 9:19). Our life should be marked by striving in our relationship with Jesus (Luke 13:24; Col. 1:29). And that spiritual progress should be evident to those around us (1 Tim. 4:15). We should be further down the road toward mature manhood now than we were six months ago. Distance matters.

But distance is not primary. For me, the constant emphasis of distance continually discouraged me. I never felt like I had made the kind of progress I needed. I lived with a sense that the Lord was disappointed with me. But over time, by God's grace, the Lord gave me a new word. Instead of distance, I began to think about *direction*.

When Jesus invites us into a relationship with Him, He invites us to follow Him. He invites us into a direction. He is the direction. Our focus is not on distance, but on Him. And as we focus on Him, we make progress. In other words, if we focus on direction, God will take care of the distance. But if we focus on distance, we might end up going a long way in the wrong direction.

God does not transform us in a day, or a week, or a year. God works on us slowly but steadily throughout our lifetime. We are disciples. We have entered into a lifelong process with Jesus. And real change in our lives happens as we simply choose, every day, to head in the right direction. This is how we walk with Jesus.

My hope is that this book will have pointed you in the right direction. And that as you choose to walk in that direction, you will look back someday and realize, by God's grace, you have gone the distance and finished the race.

Every day. One foot after another. Headed in the right direction. Eyes on Jesus. Until He takes you home. Remain faithful!

NOTES

1. Amy Morin, "Loneliness Is as Lethal as Smoking 15 Cigarettes Per Day. Here's What You Can Do about It," *Inc.* June 18, 2018, https://www.inc.com/amy-morin/americas-loneliness-epidemic-is-more-lethal-than-smoking-heres-what-you-can-do-to-combat-isolation.html. See also "The Loneliness Epidemic," HRSA, January 2019, https://www.hrsa.gov/enews/past-issues/2019/january-17/loneliness-epidemic.

2. Although many people have articulated this idea of a plow and a sword, I am indebted to Richard D. Phillips for his work on this subject in *The Masculine Mandate*. This is one of the most helpful books I have ever read on true masculinity. I recommend it to you for your careful reading.

3. Thomas P. M. Barnett, "Old Man in a Hurry," *Esquire Magazine*, July 1, 2005, https://thomaspmbarnett.com/globlogization/2010/8/21/blast-from-my-past-old-man-in-a-hurry-2005.html.

4. I am deeply indebted to Bruce Edstrom for helping see how these four aspects of our identity work together for a person's identity.

5. Warren Baker and Gene Carpenter, eds., *The Complete Word Study Dictionary* (Chattanooga, TN: AMG Publishers, 2003).

6. John MacArthur, *Slave: The Hidden Truth about Your Identity in Christ* (Nashville: Thomas Nelson, 2012).

7. Fred Hartly, *Parenting at Its Best* (Grand Rapids, MI: Revel, 2003).

8. E. M. Bounds, *The Necessity of Prayer* in *The Complete Works of E. M. Bounds* (Grand Rapid: Baker: 1990), 47.

9. Gene Getz, *The Measure of a Man: Twenty Attributes of a Godly Man* (Ventura, CA: Regal, 2004), 21.

10. Jonathan Edwards, *On Knowing Christ* (Carlisle, PA: Banner of Truth, 1990), 23.

11. G. K. Beale and Mitchell Kim, *God Dwells Among Us: A Biblical Theology of the Temple* (Downers Grove, IL: IVP, 2014), 15–28.

12. Augustine, *Confessions*, 1.1.1. Accessed online at https://www.gutenberg.org/files/3296/3296-h/3296-h.htm.

13. John Piper, *Let the Nations Be Glad! The Supremacy of God in Mission*, Third Ed. (Grand Rapids: Baker, 2010), 15.

14. www.joshuaproject.net

15. https://www.oxfordlearnersdictionaries.com/us/definition/english/zeal

16. https://www.merriam-webster.com/dictionary/zeal

17. John Stott, *What Christ Thinks of the Church* (Grand Rapids: Baker: 2003), 113.

18. http://www.cmalliance.org/devotions/tozer?id=1558

19. Saul is the Jewish version of his name, and Paul is the Greek version. After he was converted, he became the "apostle to the Gentiles," so his Greek name represents his post-conversion, Christian life.

20. Robert E. Coleman, *Master Plan of Evangelism* (Grand Rapids: Revell, 1993), 21.

21. Iain H. Murray, *The Forgotten Spurgeon* (London: Banner of Truth, 1973), 192.